Twentieth-Century Spies

Neil Root

W F HOWES LTD

This large print edition published in 2011 by
W F Howes Ltd
Unit 4, Rearsby Business Park, Gaddesby Lane,
Rearsby, Leicester LE7 4YH

1 3 5 7 9 10 8 6 4 2

First published in the United Kingdom in 2010
by Summersdale

A CIP catalogue record for this book is available
from the British Library

ISBN 978 1 40747 325 3

Typeset by Palimpsest Book Production Limited,
Falkirk, Stirlingshire
Printed and bound in Great Britain
by MPG Books Ltd, Bodmin, Cornwall

MUN

Please return / renew by date shown.
You can renew it at:
norlink.norfolk.gov.uk
or by telephone: 0344 800 8006
Please have your library card & PIN ready

5|4

1 5 MAR 2016

2 1 JUL 2016

NORFOLK LIBRARY
AND INFORMATION SERVICE

ROTATION
PLAN

CONTENTS

INTRODUCTION

This book is a survey of ten of the most interesting spy cases of the twentieth century. It does not claim to be an exhaustive account of the century's espionage, and the focus is specifically on those who spied for another country, one to which they were not attached or had no allegiance to by birth, citizenship or employment. The ten cases were chosen to illustrate the full range of motivations for spying, such as financial gain, political ideology, dissatisfaction with society or misplaced loyalty to friends or countries, as well as the circumstances that may coerce someone into committing espionage.

Spying stretches back to ancient civilisations, with various examples from ancient Egypt, Greece and the Roman Empire. One of the first major spy networks in more recent times was that organised by Sir Francis Walsingham in Elizabethan England. In the twentieth century, which saw two world wars, the Cold War and numerous other conflicts, the gathering of intelligence against enemies became more sophisticated and ruthless as the political stakes were raised and the technology of espionage developed more rapidly. There was also a massive growth of peacetime spying: knowing what your potential enemy was doing in peacetime became as important as defeating that enemy in a war. By the time that spies were being arrested within the CIA and FBI in the 1990s, the world of espionage was almost unrecognisable from that ninety years prior. The ten spy cases presented here, ranging from Mata Hari at the beginning of the century to Aldrich Ames at the end, illustrate the development of espionage and showcase the most interesting personalities involved.

The celebrity exotic dancer Mata Hari was caught up in the paranoia of World War One, when the fear of spies was suddenly pervasive. Other spies from the first few decades of the century were more defined by political ideology and its impact on political events, mainly the rise of communism and the spread of fascism. Some, such as the Cambridge Five, Klaus Fuchs and Julius and Ethel Rosenberg, were greatly influenced by political idealism, while others were more focused on their own gain, loyal to themselves and their own intellect more than anything else. As the divide between the West and the East widened, John Vassall experienced the Soviets' newly developed blackmailing techniques, and those involved in the Profumo Affair were manipulated and played largely due to their own carelessness. For Aldrich Ames, political alliances and loyalty mattered little; money was all.

It should be noted that this book includes the first in-depth analysis of the memoirs of Anthony Blunt, a member of the Cambridge Five ring of spies and Surveyor of the Queen's Pictures. His memoirs, publicly released in the summer of 2009, give Blunt's considered view of his espionage, treachery and public disgrace. As a former spy and an intellectual, Blunt is adept at not divulging incriminating details, but in the emotion of old age, in the midst of his own ruin, he gives us more than he perhaps realises, with rare honesty and emotion.

As late as 1999, a tiny elderly woman named Melita Norwood, aged 89, was exposed as a former Soviet spy, with some saying that her work for the Russians was as important as that of Kim Philby or Klaus Fuchs. This is debatable, but the frail, bespectacled lady filmed outside her cottage for the television news was far from the popular image of a spy. Her spying had been mainly done in the 1940s and contributed to the Soviet atomic effort. She was not prosecuted, as she was so old and it was so long after the event, with the Soviet Union then extinct for almost a decade. But it is also possible that any prosecution would have embarrassed the British secret services because of security lapses they allowed to happen decades before.

The importance of public opinion should not

be underestimated. The public's view of its own security is paramount in the minds of elected government officials in democratic countries, although in totalitarian regimes security information is largely kept hidden from the public. It is certainly the case that the anti-German paranoia in France and Britain led to the extreme way in which Mata Hari was dealt with, for example. Likewise, the Cambridge Five changed the way that treachery was viewed in Britain and its secret services forever, and the anti-communist feeling in the United States from the late 1940s to the mid–1980s affected greatly the attitudes of the FBI, CIA and American public opinion in general.

Throughout the twentieth century, the public's interest in espionage has been reflected in fiction and films about spies, which have been popular ever since such books as Joseph Conrad's *The Secret Agent*, Erskine Childers's *The Riddle of the Sands* and William Le Queux's novels were written before and during World War One, playing up to the anti-German feeling. Graham Greene's spy novels, which were informed by Greene's own experiences as an intelligence agent, would also later have a huge impact, as would the work of John le Carré (David Cornwell, also an intelligence agent) and Len Deighton. But perhaps the greatest influence on the way that espionage grew in the public consciousness in the West were the novels of Ian Fleming, who worked in Naval Intelligence during World War Two, and the resulting James Bond film franchise. More recently, Tom Clancy's novels have created a blueprint in the minds of the public about the CIA.

This book contains the facts about true spy cases which are often more incredible, thrilling and complex than fiction. The motivations of those who spied or were accused of spying for an enemy power in the twentieth century are often as interesting as the events themselves and key to understanding how a person may become a traitor. Childhood experiences, political and social idealism, hatred of the establishment and a keen need for adventure and thrills are among the main factors in turning to espionage for a foreign power. The promise of financial reward, entrapment by blackmail or simply propitious circumstances may also play a part in certain cases. The reader must make his or her own final judgements when it comes to motivations, with the known facts serving as tools to that end. The survey offered here is an attempt to understand the reasons why these people spied (or if they spied, in one or two cases) against the social and political world in which they lived, as well as hopefully being an interesting read too.

CHAPTER 1

MATA HARI

In the early morning of 15 October 1917, a forty-one-year-old woman was woken up in the Saint-Lazare Prison in Paris by Father Arbaux and two 'sisters of charity'. Captain Pierre Bouchardon was there too – the tall, nervous military prosecutor who had arrested the woman. Also present was her lawyer, Edouard Clunet. The woman had been sleeping, and the guards at the prison were to remark later that it was a peaceful sleep. After the sisters had roused her, the woman was told that her time had come.

'May I write two letters?' she asked. Captain Bouchardon agreed, and she was given writing materials. She wrote the letters very quickly as she sat on the edge of the bed in her cell. The letters were entrusted to her lawyer. The woman then began to get dressed. She was tall and sat down to put on her thin black stockings. Next she put her black velvet cloak over the silk kimono she had been wearing over her nightgown. She then strapped on a pair of high-heeled shoes. Her jet-black hair was braided, and she placed a black felt hat on her head. Finally she put on a pair of black kid gloves. Turning to the people in her cell, she spoke calmly. 'I am ready,' she said.

She was led out to a waiting automobile. It was just after 5 a.m., the air was chilly and fresh, and the woman would have been glad to have her heavy cloak. Paris was silent and unaware as the car made its way towards the army barracks at Vincennes. The barracks were part of an old fort that the Germans had attacked in 1870 during an earlier war with no direct connection with the Great War then raging, which had brought about the unique circumstances for the woman's imprisonment.

None of the Parisian public knew she was in the car, but many knew her name. She was now plump and in early middle age, but her face was very pretty and still possessed the quality that had transfixed so many men. Her name was Margaretha Zelle, but if anyone had been awake in Paris on that dawn, they would have known her as Mata Hari.

With an almost mythological figure such as Mata Hari, it is important to separate fact from fiction and assess the faction that lies somewhere in the middle: the legend versus reality. Some have suggested that she was the original femme fatale, a woman who was dangerous to know. This is possible, as she met her end in France, where the term 'femme fatale' originated, and her life and death certainly possessed the required notoriety. She is known as a spy and as an exotic dancer. She was no doubt the latter, and the confidante of many high-placed men, but was she a spy? And if she was a spy, what was her motivation? Or was there a conspiracy against her? The answers surely lie in her life, but after so long, is it possible to know the answer definitively? This is an especially difficult question, as Mata Hari herself liked to create her own legend during her lifetime. She laid the foundations of her iconic status solidly.

Undoubtedly she is the most infamous female spy in history. The subject of countless Hollywood films, she was perhaps most famously played by Greta Garbo in *Mata Hari* (1931). Characters obviously based on her have also appeared frequently on television, and she has been the focus of scores of newspaper articles and books. The fact is that the legend of Mata Hari has glamour, intrigue and the air of conspiracy. This all sells. She has also been a feminist icon to some women – the strong-willed woman wronged by the male dominated society in which she lived. Or was she a strong and emancipated woman who could more than hold her own against the men around her? Was she really a cold and ruthless spy who sent people to their deaths through the information that she passed or a victim of circumstance? The truth might be either, or somewhere in the middle. But there is one absolute certainty – any study of twentieth-century spies has to begin with Mata Hari.

Margaretha Geertruida Zelle was born in Leeuwarden, the Netherlands, on 7 August 1876, the second of four children of Adam Zelle and Antje van der Meulen. Adam Zelle was a milliner by trade, and ran a successful hat shop in Leeuwarden, the capital city of the northern Dutch province of Friesland. He adored his only daughter. She would say later that her father thought of her as 'an orchid among buttercups'. Margaretha was a confident child, and from a young age she enjoyed wearing colourful and outlandish clothes. She also loved to tell her friends at school fantastic tales about herself, often stories that elevated her birthright. She said, 'I was born of illustrious ancestors' and 'my cradle stood in Carminghastate', referring to a large mansion in Leeuwarden where local nobility lived. This early myth-making would develop further in Margaretha, and it would colour her personality as an adult. She was something of an exhibitionist with a love of the dramatic, and her dress, behaviour and grand claims about her past would create her legend but also work against her later. At school she was well liked, and she showed a strong flair for languages.

Adam Zelle made successful investments in the burgeoning oil industry, and so the family lived comfortably during Margaretha's early years. She attended exclusive private schools and was no doubt a well-educated child with social aspirations. The role of young women of Margaretha's class at that time was a very conventional one. She was expected to get a good education, to be able to conduct herself in upwardly mobile social circles and attract and marry a man with a steady income and good prospects; to give him children and know how to organise and run a large household. However, this usual route was thwarted for Margaretha when her father was declared bankrupt in 1889, when she was thirteen years old. Adam Zelle had made some risky speculations on the stock market and lost everything. The Zelles were forced to sell off all their furniture and move to a poor area of the city – quite a comedown from the affluent one in which they had lived until then. Adam went to Amsterdam to try to start again (or so he claimed) and left Antje, Margaretha and her three brothers behind.

Antje did not fare well bringing up the children alone with no money, and she succumbed to depression and then illness. In 1891 she died suddenly, when Margaretha was just fifteen years old. Her father returned to Leeuwarden for the funeral, but he did not take in his children again. They were separated and went to live with various relatives. Margaretha went to live with her godfather Heer Visser in the town of Sneek, south-west of Leeuwarden – but soon after, at his suggestion, went to the town of Leiden (Leyde) to train to be a

11

kindergarten teacher. The headmaster of the training school was Heer Wybrandus Haanstra, and the teachers were taught to discipline the children strongly. Margaretha's character was not well suited to the job, as she was not a natural disciplinarian.

Margaretha was not to proceed on this career path anyway. The headmaster became enamoured of her and began to make advances. It seems that she returned his attentions in a small way, and the 'romance' caused a scandal, forcing Margaretha to leave the school. How aggressively Heer Wybrandus Haanstra had made a play for her and the extent to which she encouraged him is impossible to say, but in a small Netherlands town in the late nineteenth century any whiff of an affair outside marriage was exceptionally controversial.

It is important to note here how attractive Margaretha already was to men. Basically, she stood out. She was 5 ft 5 in tall at a time when the majority of women were far shorter. She also had black hair, dark eyes and a slightly olive complexion, a rarity among the generally light-haired, blue-eyed and fairer-skinned people of the Netherlands. Some who knew her as a child thought that she might have had some Jewish or Javanese blood – Java was then part of the Dutch East Indies. Margaretha was developing into a very sensual woman, a quality that would define her in the eyes of men and in general. At that time, however, this made her life even more difficult. Her godfather refused to accept her back into his home because of the scandal, and she was forced to go and live with her uncle, Heer Taconis, in The Hague. There she helped the domestic household, but one wonders if this would have been fulfilling for a young woman approaching eighteen of Margaretha's confident personality. This confidence was no doubt strengthened by the attention given to her by men.

Her life was to change after she saw an advertisement in a newspaper, the first of many twists of fate or opportunities she was to seize throughout her life. The pattern was already forming. Her childhood experiences had forged her into a wilful and determined young woman who was learning to use her charms to get what she wanted. The fact that she had had a pampered beginning that had instilled in her a need for social prestige and the expectation of a comfortable future was fundamental to the development of her aspirations and therefore actions. The double blow that her father had lost everything and her mother had died when she was so young had forced her to become fiercely independent, even if in that age a woman needed a man to operate in respectable society. Coupled with her natural need to be admired by those around her and her capacity to invent and reinvent herself (this would be proven in coming years), she was set already on the path that would make her a legend after her death. Of course, her life would ultimately end in tragedy, and along the way there would be many intrigues, the high life and hard times to come.

The advertisement that young Margaretha, hungry for a new direction, saw in the personals column of a newspaper was to change the course of her life: 'Officer on home leave from Dutch East Indies would like to meet girl of pleasant character – object matrimony.' It was not placed by the suitor himself, but by his friend. The suitor was Rudolph MacLeod, and he was no doubt surprised by his friend's action without his consent, but when Margaretha wrote to him he decided to answer her. MacLeod was Dutch but of Scottish descent, an army officer who had received a medal. At thirty-eight, he was twenty years Margaretha's senior, and he had health problems that had brought him back to the Netherlands temporarily. MacLeod's heavy drinking would also make his health worse and was an ominous sign of what was to come.

Margaretha met MacLeod and they fell in love. His attraction to Margaretha was obvious; to her, he was a distinguished man in uniform and perhaps a passport out of her current restrictive world. Most importantly though, he was probably a replacement father figure for her own father, to whom she had been very close. Margaretha would grow into a very independent woman who was something of an opportunist and risk-taker, but she was also young and vulnerable with no money of her own. When MacLeod proposed to her, Margaretha instantly accepted.

Margaretha had told her prospective husband that both of her parents were dead as she was not sure if he would find her now poor and ageing father impressive. This was an early sign of Margaretha's ruthlessness in getting what she wanted, but it should be remembered that Adam Zelle had effectively abandoned his children. There was a problem, however: a law which stated that a female could marry at the age of sixteen but not without the consent of her parents, and not until she was thirty years old without consent. If her parents had both indeed been dead there would have been no problem, but with her father still alive, she had to get his consent. Margaretha could not wait another twelve years. She confessed to MacLeod that she had deceived him, and he forgave her. Her father then gave them his consent, and they were married on 11 July 1895, just three months after their engagement. The local gossip was that the marriage had been forced by pregnancy, but this was not the case. Their first child, named Norman John, was born on 30 January 1897.

The early signs were that the marriage was not to be a happy one. MacLeod was a heavy drinker and a womaniser, and he took to hitting Margaretha when he was in his alcoholic stupor. Domestic violence at this time was not uncommon, with many husbands acting in ways that would be unacceptable today. MacLeod's behaviour was largely caused by an obsessive jealousy which made him paranoid about his wife's loyalty; this was not helped by the fact that many men found her very attractive. Then the news came that MacLeod was going to be transferred to Java. Margaretha welcomed the news. It was her big chance to make a different life, and to fulfil her ambitious social aspirations. Java was exotic, and the young Margaretha had already developed a love and need for this. Java was to shape her as a person and bring about the greatest invention of her life: herself. Arriving in the city of Abawara with baby Norman and her husband, Margaretha was captivated by this mystical place. But MacLeod soon reverted to his old ways, and took a native concubine. There is also some evidence to suggest that MacLeod raped Margaretha more than once on Java. His jealousy had also not abated. Margaretha wrote: 'My husband won't get me any dresses because he's afraid that I will be too beautiful. It's intolerable. Meanwhile the young lieutenants pursue me and are in love with me. It is difficult for me to behave in a way which will give my husband no cause for reproaches.'

MacLeod became more and more hostile, refusing to allow Margaretha to learn the Malay language spoken on Java, probably for fear she would integrate too well (however, Margaretha secretly learned the language, using her great aptitude for linguistics). He was also abusive to their servants, and it cannot have been an easy household to live in. Then Margaretha became pregnant again. Their second child was born on 2 May 1898, a girl named Jeanne Louise, though she was usually called Non, a Malay name. Even this did not make MacLeod happy, as he had wanted another son. Soon after, MacLeod was told that he was to be made a garrison commander in Medan, Sumatra.

Their new home in Medan was a vast improvement, and MacLeod's new position meant that they had to entertain often. Margaretha was expected to be a society hostess, and she took naturally to this role. Her acting, language and reinvention skills served her well here. Erika Ostrovsky in *Eye of Dawn* said of her: 'She could reign like a queen. Dressed in the latest fashions imported from Amsterdam, a paragon of beauty and elegance, she conversed with visitors in their native language – whether Dutch, German, English or French – gave instructions to the servants in Malay, played the piano most musically, danced with unusual grace.' MacLeod felt genuinely grateful towards his wife, and life for Margaretha must have seemed to be looking up. She had found her place.

However, this hopeful turn would lead to tragedy. On the night of 27 June 1899, Margaretha and MacLeod were in bed when they heard agonising screams coming from the children's room. Margaretha raced to the room and found both children vomiting black liquid. Their bodies were in spasm and they continued to cry out in pain. MacLeod ran from the house to find a Dutch doctor but their son Norman died very quickly; their daughter was saved at the hospital. It was said that both children had been poisoned, but they could also have contracted a tropical disease. If they were indeed poisoned, it was never proved who did it, though it was rumoured that a servant whom MacLeod had treated badly might have been the culprit. Regardless, their son was dead and little else mattered.

Both Margaretha and MacLeod were grief-stricken, but they dealt with the tragedy in different ways. Margaretha would sit staring at nothing for hours while MacLeod would fly into rages, sometimes unfairly blaming his wife for their son's death (this may have been guilt on his part, especially if he believed a servant he had wronged had killed Norman). MacLeod was soon transferred back to Java, and to add to her anguish Margaretha caught typhoid. In hallucinations she saw Hindu gods (she had studied some Hindu texts). MacLeod was insensitive even when she was ill, complaining that her medicines were too expensive. Margaretha recovered, but she was now realising that there was no happy future with her abusive husband. She wrote to her father and sister-in-law, begging them to send her money so that she could go back to Europe. They both refused, advising her to be a better wife. Luckily, MacLeod himself now decided that he wanted to return to the Netherlands. Margaretha's relief was cut short when MacLeod beat her badly soon after their return and walked out, taking their daughter with him.

Divorce was not common in the Netherlands, but Margaretha could take no more. She went to a tribunal in Amsterdam and applied for a legal separation. This was granted, and the court ruled that MacLeod had to return their daughter to Margaretha and make regular monthly payments for the child's upkeep. The girl was returned, but MacLeod refused to make the payments, saying that he was too poor. He then went on to do something even more spiteful – he placed an advert in the newspapers in Amsterdam that read: 'I request all and sundry not to supply goods or services to my estranged wife Margaretha MacLeod-Zelle.' He tried to convince the public that Margaretha had deserted him. It has to be remembered that society was much more conservative at that time, and any hint of scandal attached to Margaretha would have made her an outcast. She could not find a job, and so had to return her daughter to MacLeod. This was probably what he had been aiming for.

Margaretha had to go and live with relatives again, where she was not very welcome. She must have felt helpless and frustrated. She had wanted to see Paris for some time, and somehow she found enough money to make her way there. She fell in love with the sophisticated and artistic city, but unfortunately she could not find a job either in the theatre or in modelling. With no choice but to return to the Netherlands, she went back defeated, but not for long. Through a series of tragedies and hardships, mostly not her fault, Margaretha had become a survivor by necessity; her spirits were not dampened. She knew that life had more to offer her if she could find the right situation. She felt that Paris was her future and became focused on returning there and making herself a success.

It was a new century, the twentieth century, and changes in society were happening fast. Margaretha was about to have a rebirth. It would need all of her charm, intelligence and determination. She was going to make it in a place where she would be appreciated.

To reinvent herself on her return to Paris in 1903, Margaretha took a stage name, determined to forge a performing career. She worked for a time as a circus horse rider, using the stage name Lady MacLeod. This was her entry into the world of entertainment, then considered very vulgar for a woman, but far short of the social boundaries she would eventually cross. During this time she lived a transient and financially unstable existence, moving often and living on her wits.

But more and more she wanted to be a dancer,

and to facilitate this transition she began to use the stage name Mata Hari, taken from the Malay language. On 13 March 1905, she made her debut as an exotic dancer at the Musée Guimet under her new name. She caused a sensation, which is described by Erika Ostrovsky in *Eye of Dawn*: 'The diaphanous shawls she wore as the dance began were cast away to tempt the god until finally . . . the sarong was abandoned and her silhouette, with her back to the audience, writhed with desire towards her supernatural lover . . . Mata Hari groaned and worked her loins deliriously.'

The 'supernatural lover' is the Hindu god Shiva, a statue of whom Mata Hari used in her routine, an insinuation that she was raising the power of a higher spirit when she danced. Other contemporary dancers, such as Isadora Duncan, also used Egyptian and Asian themes. Margaretha had spotted this trend and helped to pioneer it. This mixture of mysticism and eroticism was explosive, especially in 1905. Even in liberal Paris, an almost fully nude woman dancing suggestively must have been a spectacular and controversial sight. It got exactly the reaction that Margaretha, now Mata, wanted. She went on to perform in Monte Carlo, Germany and Spain, in addition to her many Paris performances to come. She was never totally nude – she felt that her breasts were too small at a time when the fuller figure was in vogue, so she wore breast-cups, and a skin-coloured body stocking shielded her pubic hair from view. But the suggestion was enough, and imaginations ran wild.

Mata Hari had arrived.

In the beginning, the legend of Mata Hari was strongly driven by Margaretha herself. Very much as an actor inhabits a role, 'Mata Hari' became Margaretha's alter ego, and Margaretha distorted the truth about her own past to create her legend. The stories of her father's bankruptcy, death of her mother, poor and unhappy teenage years, failed and violent marriage, the death of her son and loss of her daughter were never mentioned. But it should also be remembered that this is not uncommon in the entertainment world, where image is everything. Aside from her near nudity, the success of Mata Hari in the eyes of western Europeans depended on a perception of her as almost being from another world. Margaretha fuelled this perception, and after a while the legend took care of itself.

Mata Hari claimed that she was born in India to a high family, and her hair, eyes and colouring helped to support this. She elaborated further by saying that her mother had been a temple dancer and that she had died giving birth to her. She had then apparently been brought up in the Hindu temple of the god Shiva, and sacrificed to his service. Her reading of Hindu texts no doubt gave Margaretha the knowledge to back up these statements. In her 2007 book *Femme Fatale*, Pat Shipman quotes Mata Hari as saying:

My dance is a sacred poem in which each movement is a word and whose every word is underlined by music. The temple in which I dance can be vague or faithfully reproduced, as here today. For I am the temple. All true temple dances are religious in nature and all explain, in gestures and poses, the rules of the sacred texts.

For the next seven years, from 1905 until 1912, Mata Hari danced regularly and achieved a high level of fame in Europe. Her official MI5 file (KV 2/1) contains many press cuttings about her from newspapers and magazines, including the London *Evening Standard*, *The Evening News* and the *Daily Mail*, as well as French and German magazines. Many of them carry photographs of her dancing, and even in still images her exotic beauty and shimmering elegance are evident. However, by 1912 she was in her late thirties and her body was beginning to age. It was at about this time that she began to become something of a courtesan, entertaining men. Her beauty and her fame, or notoriety, as a sensual dancer were now assured. She bewitched many men. But the shrewd Margaretha who had effectively already lived several lives before starting as a dancer at the late age of almost thirty knew that she could not go on forever. It should be noted that she wrote frequent letters to her daughter during this period, but they were returned unopened by her former husband. There was even an unsuccessful attempt by Margaretha to kidnap her daughter by using one of her servants.

She had already become the mistress of the Lyon millionaire Émile Étienne Guimet, the founder of the Musée Guimet, where she had made her debut. This affair would go on for some time. Her relationships with several high-ranking soldiers and politicians from different countries, including the German Crown Prince, would cause her trouble later but for now helped pay for her luxurious lifestyle. Undoubtedly there were other courtesans in Paris living in a similar way, but at the outbreak of World War One in 1914, her connections with the French intelligence services would create the backdrop to her downfall.

Just over two months before the start of the war, on 23 May 1914, Mata Hari performed at a music hall in Germany. Some members of the audience that night lodged complaints about the indecency of her act. A German policeman called Griebel was sent to witness it and pass judgement, but he fell in love with Mata Hari and arranged to take her out. This is where the story becomes misty.

There are two camps of thought regarding Mata Hari, and both need to be explained.

One camp believes that she was guilty of being a German spy, and in this version, the German policeman Griebel did not take Hari out, but his superior, Traugott von Jagow, did. This camp also says that von Jagow was the head of German intelligence, and that he persuaded Mata Hari to spy on France for Germany. The political situation was very tense at this time, and it is possible. This view of events, held by a number of scholars, goes on to say that Hari attended a spy school in Antwerp for fifteen weeks, where she learned all the techniques of spying and was given the code name 'H-21'.

The other camp says that Mata Hari was never a German spy, and that she never went to the Antwerp intelligence school. It is also known that Mata Hari herself always firmly denied going there. What is certain is that she left Germany on 6 August 1914, two days after the war with Germany broke out. She would later say that she left so quickly because the German authorities were treating foreigners suspiciously, and as she had lived in Paris for years she was considered French, and France was now Germany's sworn enemy. She went to Switzerland, and then back to Germany because of a problem with her papers. Next she went to Amsterdam, and would travel between there and Paris in the coming months. The Netherlands remained neutral during World War One, so she was able to travel relatively easily on her Dutch passport.

It was back in Paris that Mata Hari met the man who is generally considered to be the true love of her life. He was a Russian soldier called Vladmir Masloff, and he was only twenty-one years old while she was now almost forty. She was flattered by the attentions of a handsome, much younger man, and it is possible that he was a subconscious replacement for her dead son Norman in some way. For Masloff, she was a famous and highly desirable woman whom many men coveted. However, as so often in the life of Margaretha/Mata, fate was to be cruel. Masloff was sent back to the front to fight, a brutal environment of trench warfare and heavy casualties, and there he lost the sight of an eye as a result of being gassed by the Germans. He also faced losing the sight in his other eye and was to be treated in a special military hospital at Vittel. It was in the war zone, so Mata needed special permission to go and see him there. She apparently wanted to finance for him the best medical treatment available. To gain access to her lover at Vittel, Mata became acquainted with a Frenchman called Georges Ladoux, in charge of French counter-espionage, whom she met through an acquaintance. Knowing this man would eventually lead Mata Hari to her death.

Georges Ladoux tried to persuade Mata Hari to become a French spy, as he knew that she had many contacts and that with some subterfuge she could get some information. He dangled a financial carrot, and gave her some time to think about it. She thought about it, and her decision was to accept his offer. There were probably three reasons for this: desire to gain access to her lover to help him, the perceived glamour of spying to her adventurous mind, and perhaps most importantly the financial rewards. She was a woman who expected to live in a very comfortable way, and the promise of a large, though unknown, sum of money would probably have been very attractive to her. The amount offered, and much more information about the case, will not be known until the French government's files are opened in 2017 after a hundred years, if the information is still there.

For a woman to be chosen to act as a spy was uncommon at this time, and this would be one of the reasons that Mata Hari became unique in the eyes of society. Female spies had operated in minor roles before, but such active recruitment of a woman by an intelligence service was very new then. It was only later in the twentieth century that secret services realised how useful women could be. Most men would not think that a woman could be an agent at the time of World War One. Spies were usually recruited from the military so were male, or through family connections which Mata Hari did not have. Women were often patronisingly thought too gentle and simple-minded to be spies, but this very outward unsuitability would prove to be a valuable asset for later female agents. One female Soviet agent operating in Britain in World War Two and after would comment that putting out her young son's washing on the line in the garden was a perfect cover for her espionage. But Mata Hari was not a conventional woman.

Ladoux thought hard about how best to use her, and decided that she would be most useful in Brussels. She knew a businessman there that could get her access to General Moritz von Bissing, who was in charge of the German occupation of Belgium. The plan was for her to seduce von Bissing, and hopefully get him to tell her some classified military information. Because of the disruption caused by the war, Mata Hari could not travel directly to Belgium – she had to go via Britain, Spain and Holland – and it was in Britain that her troubles began.

She was arrested as soon as her boat docked at Folkestone. In Mata Hari's MI5 file there is a physical description of her at the moment she was arrested after stepping off the boat: 'Height: 5 ft 5 in; Build: medium, stout; Hair: black; Head and Face: oval; Complexion: olive; Forehead: low; Eyes: grey brown; Eyebrows: dark; Nose: straight; Mouth: small; Teeth: good; Chin: pointed; Hands: well kept; Feet: small; Age: 39'. Under the section headed 'Peculiarities of Carriage': 'Speaks French, English, Italian, Dutch and probably German. Handsome – bold type of woman.' In the section 'Peculiarities of Dress': 'Well and fashionably dressed – brown costume with racoon fur trimming and hat to match.' There is also an official form in her MI5 file listing the luggage that she was travelling with, and it conveys a sense of the high life that she had become accustomed to. There was one small wooden box containing a gilt clock, one hat box, three trunks full of clothes, one wooden box containing two brushes and a fine china tea service, one Gladstone bag with numerous items inside, one travelling rug and a fitted lady's dressing bag.

It seems that she was already suspected of spying for the Germans. They were looking for a certain German spy called Clara Benedix, who looked a little like Mata Hari. The fact that Margaretha Zelle had already changed her name to Mata Hari only added to the suspicions of the British. Interrogated at Cannon Row police station in London by the Head of Special Branch, Basil Thompson, she of course denied being Benedix. Her MI5 file shows that she gave Thompson a list of twelve character references which included her barristers in The Hague, Holland; Captain Ladoux, Ministre de la Guerre, 282 Boulevard Saint Germain, Paris; Count van Limburg-Stirum; Henri Rudeax, an artist, residing at the Savoy Hotel, London; the Marquis de Beaufort of the 4th Lancers, Belgian Army, France.

The following is an extract of her interrogation at the police station, present in her MI5 file:

INTERVIEWER:	'Will you describe Captain Ladoux?'
MATA HARI:	'A fat man with very black beard and very black hair, and spectacles.'
INTERVIEWER:	'How tall?'

MATA HARI:	'He was tall and fat. Fatter than a man of fifty years.'
INTERVIEWER:	'Did Captain Ladoux or the other man give you any money?'
MATA HARI:	'No.'
INTERVIEWER:	'Just a promise that if you were useful . . .'
MATA HARI:	'I would not make anything out of the Russian business. If I gave Captain Ladoux plenty of satisfaction, then I would have a million.' (French francs, presumably.)

After her interrogation, Mata Hari checked into the Savoy Hotel in London, where she stayed in Room 261.

The British authorities contacted Georges Ladoux in France, and he told them to send her to Spain, where (according to her MI5 file) she stayed at the Ritz Hotel in Madrid. There is also a letter in her file concerning Ladoux which clearly shows that he was far from supportive of Hari and which sheds some light on further developments in her case. It was from the Mission Anglaise in Paris to MI5, dated 18 November 1916:

Reference to our telegram . . . of November 16, herewith a copy of a letter from Captain Ladoux on this woman. He informs us that he has suspected her for some time, and pretended to employ her, in order, if possible, to obtain definite proof that she is working for the Germans. He would be glad to hear that her guilt has been clearly established.

Some historians who believe Mata Hari to have been a German spy have suggested that she rendezvoused with the German Lieutenant Wilhelm Canaris (who in World War Two was to be the head of German military intelligence) in Spain and that he was her controller. But there is no firm evidence of this, and many have disagreed.

It was now the end of 1916, and Mata Hari did definitely make contact with another important German contact, Major Arnold Kalle. She tried to soften him into giving her some secrets to pass to the French, and he told her that he was in the process of 'trying to arrange for a submarine to drop off some German and Turkish officers in the French zone of Morocco.' She gave this information to Georges Ladoux. However, it was not fresh intelligence, and already known to the French. Kalle had set her up to see if she would take the bait. Hari also gave some 'secret' information to Kalle. It was related to the French not being content with the British handling of the Allies, and a specific morsel about the Allies wanting to make a new offensive in the spring of the next year. But this was all unclassified information – it had even been reported in the French media. And the next time that she saw Kalle, he told her that he knew that she had passed on the information about the submarine.

Mata Hari must have returned to Paris at the beginning of 1917 expecting a big pay-off from Georges Ladoux. But he paid her nothing, saying that the submarine information was valueless and that she had to do better. She would not get the chance.

Ladoux and his colleagues in French intelligence were decoding messages they had intercepted, sent by Major Kalle to his superiors in Berlin. One of them read: 'H-21 informs us – Princess George of Greece, Marie Bonaparte, is using her intimate relations with Briand to get French support for her husband's access to the Greek throne [Aristide Briand was then Prime Minister of France]. She says Briand's enemies would welcome further defeats in the war to overthrow him. Britain has political and military control of France. French are afraid to speak up. General offensive planned for next spring.'

It is almost certain that Kalle had set Mata Hari up. The French were probably most shocked that Hari appeared to have a German code name. But was this real, or just an invention by Kalle? The information in the message was not top secret, and hardly of great damage to the French and the Allied war effort. But were the French looking for a scapegoat anyway – prepared to rise to Kalle's bait for their own reasons?

At the beginning of 1917, France was deep in the middle of the war that had begun in August 1914. It was a conflict that had engulfed much of Europe, and France and Britain were waiting for the intervention and assistance of the United States. Most of the bloodiest battles of the war had been fought in France, with brutal trench warfare and gassing, with some days seeing casualties in the high tens of thousands. It was called at the time 'the war to end all wars'. At the beginning of 1917, the war had induced a state of acute paranoia in French military intelligence, and the fear of spies was endemic. The intelligence services of this modern world were new and inexperienced, which served to make them even more insecure about infiltration. The political climate in which Mata Hari returned to Paris was truly explosive.

On 1 February 1917, Germany restarted its campaign of unrestricted submarine warfare, a tactic that threatened to win it the war, mortally wounding Britain and France before the United States could intervene. Two days later, the United States severed all diplomatic channels to Germany (although the first US troops would not enter France until 26 May that year). On 6 February, German land forces were obliged to withdraw twenty-five miles (40 km) to their Hindenburg Line fortifications. A week later, on 13 February 1917, Mata Hari was arrested in Paris.

She faced seventeen interrogations by the

military prosecutor Captain Pierre Bouchardon even prior to going before a military court. The conditions in which she was held in the Saint-Lazare Prison in Paris were primitive and unclean, and she was kept in isolation from any other prisoners, allowed only fifteen minutes of exercise a day. She wrote to Bouchardon from the prison, where she would spend eight months: 'You have made me suffer too much. I am completely mad. I beg of you, put an end to this. I am a woman.' In another letter: 'I have not done any espionage in France. Let me have provisional liberty. Don't torture me here.'

Her lawyer was actually a former lover. Edouard Clunet was seventy-four and had no experience of representing anybody on a spying charge; he had previously dealt with Hari's professional affairs. She finally stood trial at the Palace of Justice in July 1917. When the public found out, a massive crowd gathered outside, a testament to her fame or notoriety. The trial did not go well for her. Public opinion was firmly against anyone accused of spying at a time of war, and the regulations of the military court were strongly on the side of the prosecution. The main evidence against her was the intercepted message, but many witnesses were called. She was painted as a promiscuous and dissolute woman by the prosecution, and her past and fame obviously did her no favours in that perception of her. But one witness for the defence did give her a good character reference. He was a high-ranking member of the French foreign ministry, and he had also been Hari's lover.

But it was not enough. Mata Hari was found guilty and ordered to pay the costs of her case. She was then sentenced: 'The Council unanimously condemns the named person, Zelle, Marguerite Gertrude [sic], as mentioned above, to the punishment of death.' Hari was shocked by the verdict, but it was in fact almost inevitable for somebody found guilty of spying in wartime. Many soldiers had been shot for cowardice and desertion.

A letter in Mata Hari's MI5 file is enlightening as it shows Ladoux's thinking:

Mission Anglaise, Paris
3 July 1917
Marguerite Zell [sic] has been sentenced to death but the sentence has not yet been carried into effect. Captain Ladoux who had the case in hand tells me that they found nothing incriminating amongst her effects and nothing to show that she had been in any way connected with espionage in England. During her interrogation she divulged nothing but Ladoux is of opinion that now she has been condemned she will probably make a statement with a view to getting her sentenced [sic] commuted, in which case it is conceivable that there would be matter interesting to MI5.

Mata Hari spent the next three months appealing for a reprieve from prison, traumatised by her coming fate. No reprieve came. On the morning that they came to take her to her death, 15 October 1917, she had slept well, but only because she had been given a sedative. When told that her final appeal for clemency had been rejected by the president, she cried out: 'It's not possible! It's not possible!'

But once the realisation of her fate had sunk in, she handled herself with dignity, saying to a nun: 'Don't be afraid, sister. I shall know how to die.'

When the car containing Mata Hari arrived at the Vincennes barracks in the early morning, the twelve men of the firing squad were ready with their rifles. Their commanding officer stood beside them with his sword out. Hari was led down to a mound of earth that towered above her and placed in front of it. She had a short conversation with Father Arbaux, and then a soldier approached her with a blindfold.

'Must I wear that?' asked Mata Hari. She was allowed to face her end without it. The men assembled, the commanding officer raised his sword, and when it came down the barrage of shots was fired. An eyewitness, Henry Wales, reported for the International News Service: 'At the report Mata Hari fell. She did not die as actors or moving picture stars would have us believe that people die when they are shot. She did not throw up her hands nor did she plunge straight forward or straight back. Instead she seemed to collapse . . . She lay prone, motionless, with her face turned towards the sky.'

The name 'Mata Hari' in the Malay language means 'Eye of Dawn', and that morning, as the first waking of the sun glistened through the clouds, Margaretha Zelle spent her last few seconds with her eyes wide open.

Mata Hari is a figure shrouded in the mists of time and intrigue, the most famous female convicted spy ever, and an icon of excitement, glamour and decadence. She is also a feminist icon, and many believe a scapegoat in the heated and deeply suspicious climate of World War One. But she was convicted of spying in wartime against her adopted country, however unfair her trial may have been. The definitive truth may never be known, but the only hope is the release of official French government documents in 2017, a hundred years after her execution, if the real story is indeed contained in those files. Biographers and historians have grappled with her life and fate for decades and, as we have seen, there are two defined camps of thought: guilty double agent or the scapegoat of duplicitous political forces.

Mata Hari's life was tumultuous, transient and lived in an opportunistic fashion. The early pampering by her father and aligned social expectations were given a huge jolt with her father's bankruptcy and her mother's early death. Reduced to near poverty and the charity of relatives and then battered by a marriage to an abusive husband, the tragic death of her son and separation from her daughter, she had no choice but to harden and survive. Her independent, imaginative and determined spirit – shown even at her death by her refusal of a blindfold – were all that got her through.

Then there was the chameleon Margaretha Zelle who became the mystical Mata Hari, one of the most famous and ingenious creations of the twentieth century. There is no doubt that she was an opportunist, and that she could be ruthless in her own way to get what she wanted. She fabricated an image and it worked for her, giving her the high standard of living that she so craved. But when she got involved with French intelligence, she was perhaps out of her depth, a courtesan courting real danger this time. She did admit to passing old and useless information to the German Major Kalle, and this undoubtedly helped convict her. Politics must be the most ruthless way of life, especially during a long and bitter war, and she took a big step too far in that direction.

Her most recent biographer Pat Shipman has claimed that Mata Hari was never a double agent at all. Was she the scapegoat of Georges Ladoux, the head of French intelligence who recruited her? Incredibly and perhaps incriminatingly, Ladoux was later arrested as a double agent himself, and would admit that it was possible that she was the victim of a hoax set up by the Germans through Major Arnold Kalle. Or was it a set-up by the Germans, capitalised on by Ladoux to divert attention from the front or from his own activities? One thing is for certain – Mata Hari was enmeshed in a web of deception. In 2001 two plaintiffs, Hari's hometown of Leeuwarden and the Mata Hari Foundation, launched a plea to the French government to have a review of her 1917 trial and conviction. A ninety-two-year-old researcher named Leon Schirmann claimed that she was framed by the French to increase morale at home and act as anti-German propaganda. Nothing definitive came from this development.

Mata Hari's execution itself was politically convenient for the French government as a deterrent to other potential spies and a way of boosting nationalist feeling when morale was flagging at that point in the Great War. She was also undoubtedly an easy target because of her extremely liberal way of life. Just as in Victorian and Edwardian England, France at this time was full of hypocrisy: the face it presented was pure and proper, but under the surface the activities of society were the very opposite. Mata Hari was a seeker of thrills and adventure, a woman of great force of personality and charisma, who used her amazing sensuality to get what she wanted in a male-dominated society. But was Mata Hari a true innocent who waded out of her depth? Or was she really a double agent, ruthlessly trying to manipulate two sides in a war for financial gain? It could be said that the legend she created herself helped to convict and kill her. One thing is for certain, however: Mata Hari was no Sidney Reilly.

CHAPTER 2

SIDNEY REILLY

Thursday, 5 November 1925 was a freezing day, perfect for a brisk walk in the woods just outside Moscow. The three men got out of the car and went into the forest. One man walked ahead. He was about 5 ft 7 in tall, well built, his jet-black hair slicked back from his forehead. His face was heavily lined. His face had lived. It told an extraordinary story.

He kept walking slowly, his breath freezing in the winter air. But he was pleased to be out of his cell.

The shot came from behind, without warning. It went into his back. An official Soviet security report would later reveal that, 'He let out a deep breath and fell without a cry.' He was finished off on the frozen ground with a shot in the chest. The two men then picked him up and put him back into the car.

It was soon announced that the man known as Sidney Reilly had been executed, but many refused to believe it. The life of Reilly had been so dangerous and eventful and his death would remain as mysterious as his life for decades to come, one of the legends of espionage. But was he truly the 'Ace of Spies'?

His name wasn't Reilly at all, of course. He was the last major spy whose provenance and activities are still covered by the mists of intrigue. This is partly because of the time in which he operated, when records were not so rigorously kept and his activity was so sporadic that it is hard to follow. But the major reason is Reilly himself. Like Mata Hari, he was the master builder of his own legend, and he undoubtedly exaggerated and perhaps invented some of his exploits. He has been the subject of cartoons, books, numerous articles, television series and films.

His sobriquet, the 'Ace of Spies', was actually given to him by his 1967 biographer, Robin Bruce Lockhart, a man who knew Reilly personally and worked closely with him, as we shall see. But this biography proved to be sensationalist, as was the 1931 biography by Reilly's own wife – apparently written by Reilly himself and completed by her – where he is called 'Britain's Master Spy'. Reilly's exploits and activities are mysterious, but recent historians have to a large extent managed to piece together a good understanding of his life.

Reilly's MI5 file is also helpful in clarifying some points, but the fact that there is a photograph in his 1920s file of somebody who looks nothing remotely like Reilly shows just how shadowy he was. Here are the facts as far as can be ascertained. He was born on 24 March 1873 as Salomon (Shlomo) Rosenblum in the Jewish-populated Kherson gubernia of Russia. His parents were Paulina (Perla) and Dr Mikhail Abramovich Rosenblum, although Salomon was brought up by his assumed father, Grigory Hersh Rosenblum, the first cousin of his biological father. He was illegitimate, as Perla and Mikhail were not married.

Kherson was in tsarist Russia, a society ruled autocratically where there were no national elections or parliament. Russia was still run on the serf system, and civil society was weak. There were also huge ethnic divisions and discontent, and as in any society, division breeds subversion. The seeds of the rise of Bolshevism (later communism) were being sown in this period and would culminate in the Russian Revolution, an epoch-defining event that would dominate much of young Salomon's later life.

There are two versions of what happened to the young Salomon Rosenblum and how he came to leave Russia. The first version is the one that appears in Rosenblum's (or, to be precise, Reilly's) posthumous autobiography, completed by his wife and published in 1931, and has been retold more than once by different biographers. It needs to be read with extreme caution, since Reilly was a self-mythologist, and although there may be a quantum or partial truth to his claims, it is likely that the truth never got in the way of a story. Still, it gives an idea of how Rosenblum/Reilly saw himself.

This first version has young Rosenblum, aged eighteen or nineteen, working in 1892 as a messenger for the illegal Russian 'Friends of Enlightenment' revolutionary group and being arrested by the tsarist Ochrana (then Russian secret police). Upon his release, he was apparently informed that his mother was dead and told about the identity of his real father. He then changed his name to Sigmund Rosenblum. Then Rosenblum made it look like he had drowned in the Odessa harbour and became a stowaway on a British ship en route to South America. Upon reaching Brazil, he went by the name of Pedro and did itinerant manual jobs until being employed as a cook on a British Intelligence expedition led by Major Charles Fothergill. When natives attacked the ship, Rosenblum picked them off on his own with a single pistol. It is alleged that for rescuing the expedition Fothergill gave Reilly £1,500 – a large sum then – and a British passport in gratitude. A nice tale but unsubstantiated.

The scenario presented by Andrew Cook in his 2002 biography *Ace of Spies* is more believable. In this second version, Rosenblum arrived in London late in 1895. This was via France, and the story here is more sordid. Rosenblum and a fellow Russian Yan Voitek were in Paris, where they attacked two Italian anarchists on Christmas Day

1895, in order to steal a large sum of money. One anarchist had his throat cut and died immediately, and the other died in the Fontainebleau Hospital a few days later. (Yan Voitek would later recount this incident to the British Secret Intelligence Service, and he would have had no reason to have lied.) The murders were reported in the French newspapers, and the description of a suspect matched Rosenblum, but he was already on his way to London, where he settled into the expensive Albert Mansions in Rosetta Street, Waterloo, using the name Sigmund Rosenblum.

On the surface, Rosenblum made his living in London by setting up the Ozone Preparations Company, a business that sold patent medicines. There was a large appetite for alternative quackery in late Victorian and Edwardian London, and Rosenblum had no medical qualifications. Incidentally, Dr Crippen, infamous for the murder of his wife, his flight and execution for that crime, also had such a business, just a few years later. Under the surface, it has been confirmed that Rosenblum was in the pay of Superintendent William Melville of Special Branch, Scotland Yard as an informer supplying information from London's immigrant community. His linguistic skills – he spoke and wrote Russian, English, French and German – undoubtedly recommended him and served him well here.

Much of Rosenblum's youth was opportunist, and one of his activities would often lead to another. Rosenblum was consciously trying to make his way socially to gain a higher status, and he was never slow at recognising his chances. It was in 1897 that he began a steamy affair with a married woman, the wife of a reverend. Suffering from a kidney infection, the Reverend Hugh Thomas was no doubt anxious to find a cure, and the patent medicines being peddled by Rosenblum must have appealed to him. A very wealthy man, Thomas was obviously prepared to part with his cash to ease his pain. In the course of their meetings, Rosenblum met the Reverend's much younger wife, Margaret, and soon began a secret liaison with her.

Within months, the ailing Thomas had written a new will (Rosenblum's medicines had clearly not worked!) and left everything to Margaret. On 11 March 1898, Thomas checked into a hotel in Newhaven with his nurse, and the next day he was discovered dead in his room. A doctor called T. W. Andrew arrived and signed a death certificate, citing generic influenza as the cause of death. Dr Andrew apparently looked very much like Rosenblum, and Andrew Cook found no trace of a doctor of that name practising in England at that time. Thomas was buried within two days of his sudden death. The nurse, who had been recruited by Margaret, was linked to the death of a former employer of hers who had been poisoned by arsenic. But the police were not suspicious, and the death of Thomas was not investigated.

Margaret went on to inherit over three-quarters of a million pounds from her husband, a huge fortune. And on 22 August 1898, Rosenblum married Margaret at Holborn Registry Office in London. With the help of Superintendent Melville, Rosenblum was able to change his name. He chose Sidney George Reilly (Reilly was the second name of Margaret's father, Edward Reilly Callahan), and this enabled him to assume a new identity as an Irishman. His MI5 file states that he was born in Clonmel, Ireland.

It is worth pondering about Rosenblum/Reilly's personality here, and the psychology that would lead him increasingly into intrigue. He was without doubt a fanatical opportunist, and somebody who was able to spot his opportunities and seize them in order to further his own financial position, status and personal power. This was a young man who had arrived in Western Europe with nothing, and used unsavoury means to get ahead.

It should not be forgotten that Rosenblum's father was a White Russian and opposed to the Bolsheviks, and that Rosenblum worked in the underground in Russia as a youth. There were some strong ideological political motives on his part that would resurface in his later activities. It could be argued that when ideology came into play, it led to his downfall (as will be discussed later), but there was always some personal profit in it for him too. Despite his recklessness, one gets the impression that Reilly always thought of himself first. In his first years in Western Europe, he was focused on getting ahead.

This was a man without limits – morally, emotionally and socially – as his later career would prove. He was coldly mercenary, and a mercenary as a spy, selling his skills and information to the highest bidder. Rosenblum/Reilly is seen by many as a template for James Bond, and one can see why. Ian Fleming himself was disingenuous about this, and was quoted as saying: 'James Bond is just a piece of nonsense I dreamed up. He's not a Sidney Reilly, you know!'

However, in Fleming's books, Bond is cold and emotionless, just like the young Rosenblum who was involved in probably the first of his murders at the age of twenty-two (the anarchists in Paris) and then in the murder of Reverend Thomas just over two years later. Both of these ruthless incidents were for financial gain; he claimed in his posthumously published autobiography to have made and lost several fortunes. So, remembering that Rosenblum/Reilly was constantly 'on the make', it is easier to understand how he was prepared to go much further than the vast majority of others. He was also a quick learner who could adapt and bounce back from setbacks quickly. Added to this, he was quick-witted, darkly handsome and attractive to women, and his risk-taking increased his attractiveness. To both women and men, Rosenblum/Reilly was a maverick and therefore exciting to be around. His blind addiction to risk and sometimes almost psychotic view of the value of human life would make him a personal fortune, a legend in his own lifetime in intelligence circles and with the wider public soon after, but would also lead to his death.

With his new identity, Reilly was given a British passport, and this was a good cover for the work in which Superintendent Melville wanted to engage him. Reilly and his wife Margaret travelled to Russia, then still under the rule of Tsar Nicolas II. Margaret stayed in the city of St Petersburg while Reilly toured around the Caucasus posing as a businessman to gain intelligence about oil deposits there, and delivered a report on his findings to the British government. He was paid for this work.

After that, Reilly and Margaret took a ship from Egypt, and he was next seen in Port Arthur, Manchuria, then in the hands of the Russians, where he allegedly acted as a double agent for both Britain and Japan. This was just before the outbreak of the Russo-Japanese War and Port Arthur was a prime target for the Japanese. Reilly and a business partner, Moses Ginsburg, bought up large quantities of provisions such as food and coal and sold them on at a much higher price. This netted them a large profit, though it is worth nothing that war profiteering was very common at the time. It was in January 1904 that Reilly had his first real intelligence success, spying for the Japanese against the Russians. Andrew Cook alleges that, along with a Chinese engineer called Ho Liang Shung, Riley stole the harbour defence plans for Port Arthur and passed them to the Japanese, enabling them to navigate through the heavily mined harbour. The ensuing battle led to very high casualties for the Russians (31,000 dead) and the Japanese death toll was far higher than even that. But Reilly and his accomplice had shown true ingenuity and daring in securing the plans. This was a foretaste of his future espionage activities. It is possible that Reilly went to Japan next (perhaps to collect payment for his services), but by June 1904 he was in Paris. There he met up with William Melville, who was by now in charge of the forerunner of MI5, the Secret Service Bureau.

As stated earlier, the activities of Reilly leading up to his intelligence work in Russia in 1918 have spawned many legends, many instigated by Reilly himself. Some of them are worth mentioning here, as there may be elements of truth to them. The 'D'Arcy Affair' of 1904 is one of these murky tales.

The British Admiralty, whose Board controls the Royal Navy, were anxious in 1904 because it was becoming clear that the main source of fuel for its ships (up to that point, coal) was soon to be replaced by petroleum. Times were changing, and as Britain did not have sufficient oil supplies, a new chain of supply had to be established. The

Admiralty discovered that William Knox D'Arcy had signed a lucrative agreement with the Persians for oil rights from Southern Persia, and was also in the process of trying to secure oil rights in Mesopotamia (Iraq) from the Turks. But it seems that D'Arcy wanted to make a profit and wished to sell these rights on, most likely to the de Rothschild family in France. The Admiralty decided that they needed to persuade D'Arcy to sell these oil rights instead to the British Government.

The story, told by Reilly and repeated by his future acquaintance and colleague Robin Bruce Lockhart in his books, was that Reilly was asked by the Admiralty to secure the rights for Britain. Apparently, Reilly managed to find D'Arcy in the South of France. Dressed as a Catholic priest, Reilly went aboard Lord de Rothschild's yacht and convinced D'Arcy to negotiate with the British Admiralty in London instead. If this is really true, then Reilly was instrumental in the founding of the giant corporation British Petroleum (BP). However, in his book *Ace of Spies*, Andrew Cook disputes that this incident took place, though it was perhaps undertaken by Reilly's boss William Melville and an intelligence officer. It could also have been achieved diplomatically around a table. However, Cook did establish that Reilly was staying on the French Riviera immediately after these events allegedly took place.

Reilly soon travelled to Brussels and then turned

up in St Petersburg in January 1905. Little of substance is known about his subsequent activities until 1909, when Lockhart states Reilly was hired by British Intelligence to get hold of German weapons plans. Germany was rearming significantly by 1909, and the British required inside knowledge of German capability. Reilly allegedly managed to get hired as a shipyard worker under the name Karl Hahn at a plant in Essen, Germany. It is also said that Reilly had undergone training in welding for this assignment at a Sheffield engineering company. He became a welder, then a member of the plant fire brigade.

It has been verified that there was a Karl Hahn working at the Essen plant in 1909, and there was indeed a fire brigade there too. Allegedly Reilly/Hahn convinced his boss in the fire brigade that plans were needed to map where fire equipment was located in the plant. These were duly drawn up and then kept in the management office for members of the fire brigade to use. Apparently, weapons plans were also stored there. Lockhart says that Reilly/Hahn broke into the office at night by means of picking the lock to find the weapons plans, but his boss caught him. Reilly strangled his boss and escaped to Dortmund with the weapons plans, tore them into quarters and then posted each part individually, in case some didn't arrive but to ensure that the overall scheme would be understood. However, some writers are very sceptical that this incident ever took place.

Many other stories exist about Reilly in these early years. One is that he was working for the Russians in April 1912, shadowing and getting to know an international arms salesman Sir Basil Zaharoff, who also worked for Vickers-Armstrong munitions. But again, no definite proof exists. There are also claims that Reilly was dropped behind German lines many times during World War One posing as a German peasant or soldier on sick leave, and that he was able to record everything he saw by memory. Again, this is possible, but cannot be proven beyond a doubt – there is certainly no record of any of this in Reilly's MI5 file.

However, the activities of Reilly for the British Secret Intelligence Service that began after the Russian Revolution are largely documented and his activities in that period factual. Some embroidery by Reilly and others still needs to be unwound, but there are sensational facts that are undoubtedly true. To understand Reilly's activities and the events which would dictate the whole course of East-West espionage, some political and intelligence background is useful here.

In 1900, the Russian Empire was the largest land empire in the world and was ruled by the tsars. The last of them, Tsar Nicholas II, who ruled between 1894 and 1917, has been described in the *Oxford History of the Twentieth Century* as a 'well meaning politically blind incompetent possessed by a dangerous nostalgia.' These years in the build-up to 1917 saw much social unrest, and the demand for change was fuelled by the country's move in the direction of industrialisation from the 1890s. Tsar Nicolas II had remained aloof and poorly connected to the reality of what was happening around him. That was how the Bolshevik Party under Vladimir Ilyich Lenin was able to take power in a bloody coup and depose the tsar in October 1917. With the murder of Nicolas II and the rest of the Romanov family in July 1918 at Ekaterinburg, the old bloodline was finished.

The Bolsheviks under Lenin established a highly centralised one-party state. They had effective communication within the party, the loyal Red Army under Leon Trotsky (established in January 1918) and an excellent propaganda machine. But the taking of power did not ensure a smooth transition; there were three years of infighting to come and a civil war. When the tsar fell, around one million people left Russia, and some of them would make up the 'White Russian' movement, which wanted to bring down the Bolsheviks by any means. Sidney Reilly would work closely with some of these exiles.

One of the key strengths of the Bolsheviks was their ability to build a myth to gain support. However, the truth in Russia between 1918 and 1924 (when Lenin died) was very painful. There was also a heavy price to pay for the new Russia, such as famine, homelessness and unemployment. It was during these fledgling years of the new order that Reilly and others, along with the White Russians, tried to capitalise on the uncertainty and overthrow the infant regime. There was a real chance that the Bolsheviks could have been toppled in this period. Millions of ordinary Russians were living in poverty and were less than supportive of the new regime. Such a vast country was difficult to manage and control, as Stalin would later prove by his collectivisation of farms that led to even more extreme poverty and the deaths of millions.

While the epoch-changing shifts of power were taking place in Russia, World War One was raging in Western and Eastern Europe between Germany and the Allies, starting in 1914. Before the October Revolution in 1917, the Allies offered enormous amounts of capital and military supplies to Russia to keep it in the war and Russia accepted. It opened up an Eastern Front against the Germans. But Lenin was anti-war in regard to Germany, and the Germans helped fund the Bolsheviks. Within two months of the Bolsheviks seizing power, Lenin closed down the Eastern Front. This worried the Western Allies a great deal: if Russia and Germany made a separate peace, the Germans would be able to focus all their resources and might on the Western Front and obviously be a greater threat. The Armistice that halted fighting on the Eastern Front was followed a few months later by the Treaty of Brest-Litovsk in March 1918, which sealed peace between

Russia and Germany and ended all hopes of Russia continuing in the war.

Russia was now effectively the enemy, and even after World War One came to an end in November 1918 its relations with the West would never be the same again. Suspicions would grow, paranoia mounted, and the Bolsheviks were increasingly seen as a threat to the West. In March 1919 the Comintern (Communist International) was founded with the chief aim of bringing about a global revolution on the Russian model. This ambitious goal would have repercussions throughout the twentieth century until the abolition of the Soviet Union, and it would be at the centre of spying activities between the East and West.

The Bolsheviks had set up their own secret police in December 1917. Known as the Cheka, its translated full Russian name explains its purpose: All-Russian Extraordinary Commission for Combating Counter-revolution and Sabotage. This was the forerunner of the NKVD, which stood for the People's Commissariat for Internal Affairs (1922–23, 1934–43), and the KGB, the Soviet security and intelligence Service (1954–91). Sidney Reilly would have deadly dealings with the Cheka and the early NKVD.

In early 1918, Sidney Reilly began to work for MI1(c), the early form of MI6, then run by Captain Mansfield Smith-Cumming, who was the first Chief or 'C'. Smith-Cumming understood the need for extreme flexibility in running an intelligence service and was quite prepared to use any methods at his disposal. He said: 'I have no use for the usual channels except in the early morning.' It is not surprising that Reilly was hired, partly because of his language skills and ability to travel in Russia (being Russian himself) and partly his extreme capacity to take risk – although this would also make him a liability.

It is known that Reilly was in Moscow in March 1918, just five months after the revolution and while the civil war was raging in Russia. For the first time in his adventurous life it is almost certain that Reilly was now being driven by more than financial gain and the basic thrill of intelligence activity. He was disturbed by the events in his home country and sincerely wanted a return to the old imperialist order. This had been one of the reasons why he had left, and his activities as a secret messenger earlier in his youth had made him a target there as a subversive. There is no doubt that Reilly was anti-Bolshevik and had been since he was a boy, and his energies were now powered by ideology as well as personal advancement. His opposition to the Bolsheviks and all that they represented was deeply ingrained. As World War One against the Germans was entering its final phase, Reilly already thought that the new Bolshevik Russia posed a far greater threat. We can see Reilly's own thoughts in this period in his posthumously published autobiography:

> Gracious heavens, will the people in England never understand? The Germans are human beings; we can afford to be even beaten by them. Here in Moscow there is growing to maturity the arch enemy of the human race . . . What is happening here is more important than any war that has ever been fought. At any price this foul obscenity which has been born in Russia must be crushed out of existence. Peace with Germany? Yes, peace with Germany, peace with anybody. There is only one enemy. Mankind must unite in a holy alliance against this midnight terror.

Reilly's code name with British Intelligence was ST – 1. On 7 May 1918 Reilly walked up to the gates of the Kremlin and asked for an audience with Lenin. He said that he was an envoy representing the British Prime Minister Lloyd George, which was definitely untrue. Quite what Reilly was hoping to gain from a direct meeting with the Russian revolutionary leader is unclear, but it certainly shows that he had great courage. Anyway, his request was not granted. But what followed would become the centrepiece of the Reilly legend.

It would become known as the Ambassador's Plot, the Envoys' Plot or the Lockhart Plot, in reference to the junior British diplomat called Robert (Robin) Bruce Lockhart, who would later go on to publish books about Reilly and more than anybody nurture his legend as the 'Ace of Spies'. Lockhart had links to British Intelligence, and may well have been an agent too. Lockhart and Reilly met clandestinely with General Boris Sakinkov, a leading member of the anti-Bolshevik organisation the Union for the Defence of the Fatherland and Freedom (UDFF), which had thousands of members ready to fight to destabilise the new regime. There were also international political contacts made, with Reilly and Lockhart having dealings with the intelligence arms of the United States and French consulates in Moscow (Paris was now the home of key members of the White Russian movement) as well as a British naval attaché, Captain Cromie. Reilly himself was posing as a Turkish merchant, Mr Constantine. Reilly and the others were plotting an anti-Bolshevik coup of the highest order. They knew that the leaders of the new Russian government were still unsteady in their grasp of power, and the only chance of toppling the Bolsheviks would involve attacking the very top echelons.

But in reality, this attempted coup was doomed from the start. According to the Mitrokhin Archive, which shed light on many Russian intelligence activities of the century, the Cheka instigated the whole plot by use of an agent provocateur. An anti-Bolshevik named Shmidkhen convinced Reilly, Lockhart and the French consul-general that Colonel Eduard Berzin, a commander of a Latvian regiment based in the Kremlin, was ready to lead an anti-Bolshevik uprising. The Latvian regiment was in charge of security in the Kremlin itself, and so Reilly and Lockhart knew their support would give any coup attempt a far greater chance of success. What they did not know was that Shmidkhen was really a Cheka agent called Yan Buikis and that Colonel Berzin was also a member of the Cheka. Reilly gave Shmidkhen 1,200,000 roubles to finance the coup, at least partly funded by British Intelligence.

The coup was a classic example of Reilly's audacity and addiction to high risk. The first plan was for Reilly personally to lead a Latvian group of troops and seize Lenin, Trotsky and other Bolshevik leaders by force and then execute them. The second scheme was to seize Lenin and Trotsky, take off their trousers and then parade them through the streets of Moscow to humiliate them and make them objects of ridicule. Other events would intervene before either plan could be put into operation.

On 30 August 1918, Moisei Uritsky, the head of the Cheka in Petrograd, was assassinated, and on that same day Fanya (Dora) Kaplan made an assassination attempt on Lenin. The reaction of the Cheka was as iron-fisted as would be expected.

This was the beginning of what became known as the 'Red Terror'; thousands of political opponents of the Bolsheviks were rounded up and executed. Russia was still in the middle of a civil war, and the Bolsheviks were taking no chances. Dzerzhinsky ordered the Cheka to shut down the Lockhart Plot too. Captain Cromie was confronted at the British embassy in Moscow, and when he put up a fight, he was killed. The Cheka arrested Lockhart, but he was later released in a spy swap with a Russian spy, Litvinov, who had been seized in London in a tit-for-tat arrest. Three female accomplices were arrested, at least one of whom, Olga Starzheskaya, was also Reilly's mistress.

As the Mitrokhin Archive reveals, there was an announcement made by the Cheka on 2 September 1918. This gloried in the quelling of the attempted coup, but of course made no mention that the Cheka itself had been instrumental in creating it. It claimed to have 'liquidated . . . the conspiracy organised by Anglo-French diplomats . . . to organise the capture of the Council of people's Commissars and the proclamation of military dictatorship in Moscow.'

Reilly had been identified as a leader of the coup, but he managed to escape to Finland by train on a Baltic German passport with the help of a Military Intelligence associate, Captain George Alexander Hill, and then to Sweden by ship, from where he made his way to London. Once in

London, in early November 1918, Reilly and Hill were debriefed by 'C', Mansfield Smith-Cumming himself. Reilly was awarded the Military Cross (MC) for his services in Russia, and Hill a Distinguished Service Order (DSO). Reilly would officially receive his MC on 22 January 1922, but as we will see he wasn't in London to collect it in person.

Back in Russia, the Cheka was claiming a victory of great magnitude in the suppression of the Lockhart Plot. However, the reality was that the Lockhart Plot and others like it were organised by diplomats and maverick agents such as Reilly, and were not backed solidly by capitalist governments. These attempts sometimes showed an almost comic 'boys own' spirit of adventure instead of clinical realism.

The Russians mounted a Revolutionary Tribunal and Reilly was sentenced to death *in absentia*, the sentence to be carried out if he were ever caught on Russian soil again. After his debriefing, Reilly was able to enjoy a short period of leave before Mansfield Smith-Cumming sent him back to Russia. It was to be far from Moscow this time, however. Captain Hill would accompany Reilly on this mission but play a subordinate role. They would be sending intelligence from South Russia from December 1918 until March 1919. The brief was to gather relevant information about the coast of the Black Sea that could be used by the British at the Paris Peace Conference, set to begin on 18

January 1919. Hill was also gathering information about Russian aviation strength for British Military Intelligence.

This area of South Russia, between Sevastopol and Odessa, was home to a great deal of fragmented anti-Bolshevik activity and was therefore fertile ground for intelligence. Reilly would file twelve reports during those four months, mainly his impressions of political allegiances and strengths. They do show that as a native Russian himself he understood the complexities of the region. For example, his report of 11 January 1919 shows that his views about the tactics and resources needed to bring about a possible destabilisation of the Bolsheviks had drastically changed since the Lockhart Plot just months earlier. Reilly says:

> People think that in order to pacify Russia, all one has to do is to take Moscow. To hear again the Kremlin bells would, of course, be very pleasant, but we cannot save Russia through Moscow. Russia must be re-conquered as a whole.

Reilly reported that the Red Army was estimated to have around 400–500,000 men at its disposal and that by the spring of 1919 this could grow to a force of a million. These were formidable numbers, but Reilly felt that the Red Army was inferior to the established and well-equipped armies of the Allies; suppressing it would not be too difficult, if the right support was given.

Overall, the intelligence that Reilly gathered was balanced and informative, and it showed that he had a shrewd mind that understood politics when he wasn't hatching incredible schemes. The picture he paints of the new regime is one of brutality and ruthlessness. In a report from South Russia on 17 January 1919, Reilly relayed the story of Rebecca Albam. She was a university student who had been arrested for subversion, but then cleared by court martial: 'Under the guise of fighting socialism a number of glaring administrative crimes have been committed . . . her corpse [Rebecca Albam's] with her head smashed in by rifle butts has been discovered in a field'. She had been murdered en route to exile.

The new government was a machine that was vastly at odds with its image of being 'for the people'. It is necessary to understand that the Bolsheviks were fighting the socialists in Russia at this time. The Bolshevik was a far more extreme party than the opposition Socialist Revolutionary Party. Suppression was achieved by the Bolsheviks at any cost in those early days of the Red Terror and would continue later under Stalin in the Great Purges. Like any totalitarian regime, this one could survive only by maintaining absolute power.

Reilly was not a model intelligence agent, however: his ego would always get in the way of his activities and cloud his judgement. Another intelligence agent operating in Russia in 1918–19, Paul Dukes, was a truly effective agent who fulfilled his brief and was later knighted for his efforts. A master of disguise, Dukes worked under many aliases, and photographs of him from this period in different guises are truly remarkable (he is unrecognisable as the same man). So there were agents who were prepared to take the kind of extreme risks that Reilly did but who did not involve themselves in outlandish schemes.

During his time in South Russia, Reilly became far more realistic about what it would take to achieve the overthrow of the new Russian regime, but he still pictured himself at the centre of the fighting. Reilly was a fan of Napoleon Bonaparte and collected Napoleon memorabilia as a hobby, and this perhaps goes some way in explaining his own ambitions – he wanted personal power and glory. This desire would grow into a form of narcissism and megalomania, traits highly incompatible with those needed for intelligence work for an established intelligence service. An agent like Paul Dukes saw himself as a cog in the wheel of the service, providing invaluable intelligence but not overreaching himself. Reilly was too much of a 'lone gun'.

During the next few years, Reilly continued to involve himself in schemes with White Russians in exile abroad. But as Andrew Cook asserts, he was fired from the British Secret Intelligence Service in 1921, and this seems to have been because of his unreliability and habit of being a 'rogue operative'. Reilly had officially been in British Intelligence for only about three years, although of course he had worked for Special Branch beforehand. But he had won a prestigious Military Cross, and had been valued highly by Mansfield Smith-Cumming at one time. Cook thinks that Reilly was given the Military Cross largely due to his activities in South Russia around Christmas and New Year 1918–19, but the espionage historian Richard Deacon has written that it was because of his secret activities in World War One (it has been claimed that Reilly was parachuted behind German lines many times, but there is not definitive proof of this).

The plots that Reilly got himself involved in during the early 1920s had no official connection to British Intelligence at all, but he was still associating with other agents, no doubt. The schemes were planned in Europe, especially in Paris, but little actual action took place. By now, Reilly was on to his third wife, having left Margaret, and his second wife Nadine Massimo. In 1923, he married Pepita Bobadilla, a well-known actress. She certainly loved him and must have been very tolerant to deal with his growing narcissism. But Reilly had a magnetic personality and such people often get those closest to them to put up with a great deal. Reilly's ruthless streak should not be forgotten either: at least one of his marriages is thought to have been bigamous.

It was Pepita who would publish Reilly's auto-biography after his death, although it would be withdrawn from sale because of the threat of legal action from the British government. In the second half of this book, Pepita Reilly gives her own impression of her husband and the murky world he had inhabited (although she felt that he was still alive). Reilly in his last years comes across as very cynical and almost paranoid (Pepita herself had taken to carrying a gun). Pepita reports Reilly as saying to her: 'The difficulty of this game is that you never know who is with you and who is against you. Many agents are taking the pay of both sides.' But was Reilly himself ever a double agent? He is thought to have spied for Britain, Japan and perhaps Germany at various times, but it has never been established if he was in the pay of more than one nation at once.

There is also speculation that Reilly was involved in the infamous case of the Zinoviev Letter. The letter was dated 15 September 1924, and was addressed to the British Communist party, and apparently written by Zinoviev, the president of the Communist International, a Bolshevik organisation set up to bring about a global revolution. The letter instructed the British communist party to mobilise its members to prepare for a British revolution by using their contacts in the military and within the Labour Party, then in power. The letter appeared in British newspapers on 25 October 1924, just four days before the general election. It triggered anti-communist paranoia and was largely blamed for the Labour Party losing the election and the Conservative Party coming in. It was later found that the letter was a forgery, written by Russian exiles in Berlin. It must be asked whether the Russians would really want to risk losing their foothold of sympathy in Britain by the Labour Party losing power.

Reilly was thought to have been involved in informing British Intelligence of the existence of the letter, and this is highly likely, as he had many contacts amongst Russian exiles who wanted to sabotage any chance of Britain forging links with Russia, whether politically or through trading agreements.

The real question is whether Reilly knew it was a forgery but still alerted British Intelligence to it, fearful of the possible threat of communist infiltration, or whether he convinced himself that it was the real article and was genuinely disturbed by the implications. Phillip Knightley has written that the former explanation was more likely but for the reason that Reilly and SIS knew that the letter was forged but went ahead anyway. Knightley is supported by the leading espionage historian Christopher Andrew, who has said that this claim cannot be totally discounted. There was no love lost between SIS and the British Labour Party at this time; it is now known that if it gained power, Labour was planning to suspend SIS and declassify its files. This would have been a strong motive for SIS, with the help of Reilly, to discredit the Labour Party and damage its election chances.

Whatever the truth is about how the letter was taken seriously and made public, it is likely that Sidney Reilly had a hand in it somewhere. What is absolutely certain is that Reilly was again having dealings with General Boris Sakinkov, who had been involved in the Lockhart Plot. A leading White Russian and Socialist Revolutionary, Sakinkov was still trying to bring down the Bolsheviks and was still active to this purpose in exile in Paris. He had set up the People's Union for Defence of Country and Freedom (NSZRiS) in 1921. The NSZRiS had a spy network inside Russia, and Reilly had much contact with Sakinkov and his activities. But the Cheka had kept tabs on Sakinkov and soon an undercover agent within the NSZRiS managed to break the organisation. They then infiltrated Sakinkov's inner circle with another mole posing as an anti-Bolshevik, and Sakinkov sent one of his key men, Colonel Pavlovsky, to Russia to hold secret talks with an imaginary anti-Bolshevik faction in 1923.

The Soviet Security and Intelligence Service (OGPU) had just been set up, and it broke Pavlovsky. It then used him to persuade Sakinkov to come to Russia himself. It was a classic subversion tactic. On 15 August 1923, Sakinkov and a group of sympathisers entered Russia and were quickly arrested by the OGPU. According to the Mitrokhin Archive, at a show trial engineered by the Bolsheviks, he made a statement to show everyone that he had been broken, stating that he recognised only Soviet power and that any Russian patriot should do the same and back the peasant workers.

After the show trial, Sakinkov was sentenced to fifteen years in prison, but he would not live long. An OGPU officer was put in his cell and managed to get even more information from him over some months. After this, there is an account saying that he fell from a high window, but it is highly possible that he was pushed.

The death of Boris Sakinkov, a close friend and associate, must have upset and shocked Reilly, who was already paranoid. Reilly's MI5 file states that a certain M. Burtzev had had a 'telephonic conversation' with Reilly soon after Sakinkov had left Paris for Russia, although the file reports that this was in July 1924, not a year earlier, in July/August 1923, as has since been established. It reads:

> Reilly in an agitated voice went on: 'A terrible thing has happened. Of course you know what it is about. A telegram has been received from Russia, but its contents are clearly false. It talks about him having acknowledged the Bolsheviks at his trial.'

It must have been a great shock to Reilly to hear that Sakinkov, anti-Bolshevik to the core, had been broken by the OGPU, who had obviously employed brutal methods or threats to achieve this. No greater warning could have been given to Reilly, but if he was paranoid he was also prone to fantasy by this point. The Mitrokhin Archive states that one of his secretaries, Eleanor Toye said: 'Reilly used to suffer from severe mental crises amounting to delusion. Once he thought he was Jesus Christ.' Whether Reilly was delusional or just thought that he was invincible, he did not heed the warning. He may have created such an impregnable fantasy world to protect himself from his paranoia – some of it triggered by reality – that he was no longer thinking logically. Put simply, Reilly had built up a picture of himself as the 'Ace of Spies' and this was no doubt caused by symptoms of mental illness.

The Cheka and the OGPU were not finished with Reilly; there was still a 1918 death sentence awaiting him in Russia. Although the Mitrokhin Archive states that 'Reilly had become a tragicomic figure whose hold on reality was increasingly uncertain', the OGPU still saw him as a grave threat, and with some reason – he was still continuing his contacts with the White Russians in exile. Just like Boris Sakinkov, Reilly would be the victim of an elaborate trick.

Operation Trest (or Trust) was supposed to be a cover name for the Monarchist Association of Central Russia, which by definition was anti-Bolshevik. It was actually a deception set up by the OGPU that ended up running for six years.

An OGPU officer called Aleksandr Yakushev was operating undercover as a Russian foreign trade representative and managed to entrap key anti-Bolsheviks with a plan to mount an uprising within Russia. Notable people to be deceived were Grand Duke Nikolai Nikolayevich, the cousin of the murdered tsar, and General Aleksandr Kutepov, a leading White Russian, plus Sidney Reilly.

By this time, Reilly had come to the conclusion that the best way to upset the balance of power in Russia was to penetrate it and develop a clandestine network. The opportunity presented by The Trust, as the organisation was known, must have seemed too good to miss. Despite the warning of Sakinkov's entrapment, on 26 September 1925 Reilly was lured across the Russian border from Finland. He was met by supposed members of The Trust, who of course were really OGPU officers. One of these officers later recalled his first meeting with Reilly on that day, as Andrew Cook recounts in *Ace of Spies*: 'The first impression is unpleasant. His dark eyes expressed something biting and cruel; his lower lip drooped deeply and was too slick – the neat black hair, the demonstrably elegant suit . . . Everything in his manner expressed something haughtily indifferent to his surroundings.' It is true that a photograph of Reilly from the 1920s shows a deeply lined face and a shrewd, cynical expression. Years of living on his wits and the resulting paranoia had taken their toll.

Reilly was captured and taken to the Lubyanka Prison in Moscow and seen by an official called Roman Pilar, who had also been instrumental in the arrest of Boris Sakinkov. Pilar reminded Reilly about the 1918 death sentence hanging over him. After that, Reilly's interrogation began. According to the biographer Andrew Cook, Reilly was not physically tortured in the notorious prison but underwent psychological torture in the form of 'mock execution scenarios' to soften him up. Cook also claims that Reilly did not break under interrogation and reveal any secrets to the Russians. But the Mitrokhin Archive shows otherwise: 'His KGB file contains a probably authentic letter to Dzerzhinsky dated 30 October 1925, in which he promised to reveal all he knew about British and American intelligence as well as Russian émigrés in the West.' This is not unlikely, of course, when it is remembered how quickly the OGPU broke Sakinkov.

The operative to the end, Reilly was making notes about the OGPU interrogation techniques being used on him on cigarette papers in his cell, and these were later discovered. He probably knew that if he managed to escape the notes would be valuable to British Intelligence (and perhaps saleable).

It was less than a week after the letter to Dzerzhinsky is dated, on 5 November 1925, that Reilly was taken for a walk in the Moscow woods. Perhaps the fact that he was shot in the back is a sign of the respect that the Russians had for him, instead of having him face a firing squad. There is a photograph of Reilly's corpse, and it does appear to be him.

The MI5 File on Reilly shows that the fact of his death and the deception of Operation Trest was known in 1927, and that others were shot in 1925. However, because this information was not made public, the myths about Reilly still being alive continued to circulate. His MI5 file contains a Foreign Office report dated 3 October 1927 that reads:

The name of a certain Reilly, alleged organiser of terrorist acts in the USSR and a Captain in the British army, has constantly appeared in the Moscow press. It was alleged that the five arrested individuals had come over to the USSR to execute Reilly's plan of blowing up factories, bridges, newspaper offices, assassinate prominent Communists etc. and that Reilly in turn had been working under the immediate supervision of the British Intelligence Service. The official press in its mad desire to discredit His Majesty's Government in the eyes of the Russian people stopped at nothing: In 1925 the Soviet press published an official statement to the effect that a certain Captain Reilly of the British Army, an alleged spy, was arrested by the GPU and finally shot.

However, in the same MI5 file, there is an allegation reported on the same date that Reilly was still alive in 1926: 'Mr Brunovski, who was in prison at the time, and has since returned to Riga, has published an article in the 'Pondelnik' of the 26th inst. In which he states, on the authority of a fellow-prisoner, that Reilly was alive in the hospital of the Butyrski prison in the first part of the year 1926.'

Reilly's last wife Pepita was also convinced that he was still alive and wrote to Winston Churchill on 13 December 1927 to get some information about her husband. She was obviously still under the impression that Reilly had gone to Russia on the orders of British Intelligence. The reply from Churchill's office was equivocal:

Mr Churchill desires me to acknowledge the receipt of your letter of the 13th December, and to say that it appears to have been written under a complete misapprehension. Your husband did not go into Russia at the request of any British official, but he went there on his own private affairs. Mr Churchill much regrets that he is unable to help you in regard to this matter because according to the latest reports which have been made public, Mr Reilly met his death in Moscow after his arrest there.

The legend of Sidney Reilly would not die with him.

Sidney Reilly was a man who thrived on risk and adventure, for personal gain, fame and thrills. His early life shows that he was prepared to use any means necessary to get what he wanted out of life. When this compulsive opportunism and ability to manipulate dangerous situations to his own advantage was married with intelligence activities in an official capacity with Special Branch from 1898, and until he parted company with MI1 (c) in 1921, he was an agent of some effectiveness. All accounts of Reilly are of a man who was extremely shrewd in the early years of his career but less so later, a survivor and a ruthless operator. But what were his true key motivations?

If he did indeed undertake dangerous missions for Britain behind German lines in World War One then he was a valuable part of the Allied war effort, but this cannot be confirmed beyond doubt. He did have the rank of captain in the British Army, and this must have been earned through service, due to his background. Russian by birth, he was undoubtedly virulently anti-Bolshevik, as his own memoirs and reports from South Russia testify. There was more to his struggle against the Bolsheviks than the clamour for money, status and power. He had become a man with a cause, a man who saw the hypocrisy and the true brutality of the communist regime very early. Perhaps for the first time, political motives and a burning hatred of Bolsheviks and communism drove Reilly, rather than just his own self-advancement. His knowledge and understanding of that regime was portentous, and much of what he said proved to be true, as Lenin gave way to Stalin and then the long Cold War. The Cheka and the OPGU would morph into the KGB later, and Reilly's warnings of 1918–25 would become very real.

But is this view of Reilly as a man with political convictions winning over self-interest true? There is no doubt that ideology played a large part in his motivation in Russia, but the desire for the advancement of his own position was still present. All of his schemes had him at the centre of the action – he was always in a position of power in the planned execution of uprisings. The romantic notion that Reilly was a man who died purely for his beliefs is plainly simplistic and untrue.

Reilly possessed many of the traits that make a good agent. He was brave, quick-thinking, flexible, able to gather and assimilate intelligence quickly, with the drive and tenacity to go that extra distance to get what he needed. But his bravery and tenacity and propensity for blatant opportunism also worked against him as a spy. He could take unnecessary risks and his ego often clouded his judgement. By 1921, Mansfield Smith-Cumming obviously felt that Reilly was no longer an effective agent for British Intelligence. And over the next four years until his death, Reilly would continue to embroil himself in incredibly dangerous schemes. Considering that he knew the true strength of the Bolsheviks by that time, could he realistically believe that a small network would overthrow a huge, highly organised regime, especially now that the civil war was over?

Reilly may well have become a fantasist who had dangerous delusions. Was his secretary telling the truth when she said that he had a Jesus complex? Could he have perhaps identified with his hero Napoleon a little too closely and in an unhealthy way? Reilly may have thought himself almost invincible by this time, as he had survived so much. Why would a man of Reilly's former judgement and shrewdness fall into the trap of The Trust set by the OGPU, especially after his friend General Boris Sakinkov had already fallen victim to the regime? This will never be known with certainty, but it can be said that Reilly was showing signs of extreme stress by his final few years. The constant strain and paranoia had stretched and almost broken his nerves, perhaps so much so that he was suicidal in his bravery. Perhaps Reilly simply did not have the mental balance to maintain a long espionage career for an established service.

Was Sidney Reilly the 'Ace of Spies'? The answer has to be no. He led an incredible life and was an extraordinary man. But he was not the most successful British spy of the early century (this title could perhaps go to Sir Paul Dukes). He is definitely the most legendary, but the overall tally of his espionage success is not enormous, since so much of his time was spent on increasingly wild plots with no official sanction or real chance of success. Reilly was a hardened opportunist, near confidence trickster and skilled spy with psychological limitations. He lived by the sword and died by the blade of the Bolsheviks. And the insidious Bolshevik threat that Sidney Reilly warned about was soon to become a reality by means of the Communist International (Comintern). It would establish a Ring of Five that would reach so high within the British establishment that it is almost impossible to believe.

CHAPTER 3

THE CAMBRIDGE FIVE

It was approaching midnight on Friday, 25 May 1951, on a darkened quay in Southampton, England. A ship called the *Falaise* was docked and ready to depart for St Malo, France. It was a routine trip, carried out daily by timetable.

But that night a car screeched to a halt close to the quay. There was no time to find the car park. It really could have been a matter of life and death. Two men got out of the car and ran towards the *Falaise*. One was tall and slim and the other shorter. Just as they were mounting the gangway, a quayside porter called from behind.

'What about your car?'

'We'll be back on Monday!' replied the shorter man.

The two men would soon be known as 'the Missing Diplomats'. They were also two members of what the Russians called 'The Magnificent Five'. The boarding of the *Falaise* that night would have massive repercussions in Britain and the United States. Nothing in Anglo-American intelligence circles would ever be the same again.

It all began over twenty years before at Cambridge

University, which along with Oxford University was a rite of passage for members of the British establishment in the 1930s. Now over eight hundred years old (founded in 1209), it is made up of cloistered colleges. Trinity College was founded by Henry VIII in 1546, becoming the largest college of the university. Its website boasts: 'Princes, spies, poets and prime ministers have all been taught here.'

In the autumn of 1929, just as the Wall Street crash was about to happen, Harold Adrian Russell Philby, known as 'Kim', arrived at Trinity College to read history. He was seventeen years old and had attended Westminster School, a public school in London. Philby was born on 31 December 1911 in the Punjab province of India to Harold St John Bridger Philby and Dora Johnston. His father gave him his nickname 'Kim' from the novel of that title by Rudyard Kipling, being a fan of the author. St John Philby was a noted Arabic scholar, businessman, archaeologist and adventurer. He was working for the Indian Civil Service (where he apparently met Kipling) when his son was born, and later held several important postings in the Middle East and had extensive business dealings there. He had converted to Islam by the time that Kim entered Cambridge. Dora, Kim's mother, was the daughter of a civil engineer based in India, and Kim had three sisters. But it was St John Philby's strong personality and maverick tendencies which made the biggest impact on Kim.

Contemporaries have attested that Kim Philby was handsome and highly intelligent; although academically he did not distinguish himself at Cambridge, his mind diverted by other activities, mainly political. But he had a stutter that crippled him on occasion, and made him less gregarious than he should have been, although this didn't stop him being very attractive to women or hinder him in his ambitions. He had a very quick analytical mind with a natural shrewdness, disguised by a modest and self-deprecating humour.

Another student soon to join Philby at Trinity College was Guy Burgess, who arrived on a scholarship to read modern history in the autumn of 1930, although he was over a year older than Philby. Guy Francis de Moncy Burgess came from a naval family; his grandfather had been an admiral and his father an officer in the Royal Navy. His father died when Guy was thirteen, and consequently Guy had a very close relationship with his mother, Eva. Burgess had been to Eton and then to Dartmouth Naval College for a short spell, to follow in the footsteps of his father and grandfather. But he disliked Dartmouth, and he left for Cambridge.

A big and irrepressible personality, opinionated, funny, irreverent and academically brilliant – he was better read than many of his tutors and was already a Marxist at the age of nineteen (a fact that he wasn't shy in telling people) – Burgess was to quickly become a legend at the university. He was glamorous and boyishly handsome, and he could back his style with substance by having an absolutely first-rate if rather volatile mind, as his friend Anthony Blunt would later comment. He no doubt made a big impact on the younger Philby.

In 1931, another student arrived: Donald Maclean. Very tall and slim with wavy blonde hair, he was reading modern languages at Trinity Hall, a smaller college than Trinity and less famous. Born in 1913, Maclean was two years younger than Burgess and one year younger than Philby. Although he went to an English public school and his family lived in England, Donald came from a high Scottish Highland family. His father, Sir Donald, was a Labour politician, and the younger Donald grew up surrounded by liberal, left-wing views. When the son arrived at Cambridge University, the father was a cabinet minister in Ramsay MacDonald's government (as president of the Board of Education). Sir Donald Maclean would suddenly die in June 1932, leaving his son devastated.

John Cairncross was also born in 1913 and was from Lesmahagow, Scotland. He had previously studied at the University of Glasgow and taken degrees in French and German at the Sorbonne in Paris before entering Trinity College to read modern languages on a scholarship, later than the others. His brother would become the eminent economist Sir Alexander (Alec) Kirkland

Cairncross. Intellectually bright with no small amount of vanity and arrogance, John would later write a book saying that intellectually brilliant men are prone to polygamy, as a woman would rather have a percentage of a first-rate man than the whole of a mediocre one. The novelist Graham Greene playfully acknowledged this as 'a book which will appeal strongly to all polygamists'.

Anthony Blunt, born in 1907, was older than the others and had been at Cambridge since 1926. Tall and thin, aristocratic in bearing, he was the son of a priest and a distant relation of the Queen (third cousin, once removed). His father became a chaplain in France when Anthony was four years old, and so Anthony lived there until he was fourteen, when he entered Marlborough College. At school his best friend was the poet Louis MacNeice (who would become famous along with W.H. Auden, Stephen Spender and Christopher Isherwood in the 1930s and 1940s). Blunt became a don at Cambridge, elected to a fellowship in 1932, specialising in the history of art. Aloof and outwardly austere (this would increase with age), he was also very intellectually gifted. Being older than the others, at the beginning he was looked up to by them. Blunt formed a very close friendship with Guy Burgess at Cambridge.

All five of these men were born into relative privilege with very respectable backgrounds. The expectation on them would have been to pursue careers within the establishment, and this is precisely what they would go on to do – although covertly at the expense of the established order they were outwardly serving. So why and how did these five men become Soviet agents at Cambridge University and soon after, earning them the moniker of the Cambridge Five?

There were several major reasons for intellectual youth at Cambridge University to be drawn to communism at this time. Firstly, there was the British political situation. The failure of the Labour government and its consequent huge defeat in the 1931 election was compounded by Prime Minister Ramsay MacDonald's perceived betrayal of the values of the left. MacDonald had lost control of the economy during an international depression, but his most venal sin in the eyes of those on the left was that he had compromised his values by reaching an agreement with the Conservatives and Liberals in August 1931. The pain of this perceived betrayal was made more acute as MacDonald was one of the founders of the Labour Party. There was consequently profound disillusionment among left-leaning intellectual youth, typified by many Cambridge students. Having arrived at university from public schools where they had been sheltered, they began to see real life. As the first part of the old adage says: 'If you are not a revolutionary in your youth you have no heart.' With the instigation and expert manipulation methods employed by the

Comintern (Communist International) and Russian intelligence, students such as the Cambridge Five were ripe for recruitment.

Secondly, there was the economic Depression. The Wall Street crash of 1929, seen by many young intellectuals as an exposure of the folly of capitalism (which has some familiar echoes today) was followed by five years of mass unemployment. At its worst, there were three million unemployed in Britain, twelve million in the United States and six million in Germany, a high number considering the total populations of those countries in the early 1930s. This added fuel to the feeling that capitalism was doomed. The closure of coal mines, steel plants and shipbuilding yards meant that there were many hunger marches through Cambridge, and at least three of the five future spies went on them in support. There was also the new means test (which minutely tested the financial means of people), cuts in wages and employee benefits and general disregard for the working class. The Comintern exploited this disillusion, especially as Russia was obviously not affected by the Depression, although suffering its own political turmoil. For young men such as the future Cambridge spies, the theory of Marxism and a communist state was probably a very attractive alternative to the brutality of capitalism.

Thirdly, there was the international political situation. Many thought that communism was the only way to fight the growing threat of fascism.

But while Hitler had designs on both Western and Eastern Europe, Stalin had designs on Eastern Europe, and the Bolshevik vow made in 1918 to bring about a global revolution was still a strong ambition. Efforts to recruit and place the Cambridge Five in key positions in British Intelligence and the Foreign Office would give them a firm foothold.

It is easy to see how they might be attracted to the cause, but what made the Russians choose them, and how were they recruited? As we saw in the previous chapter, the Comintern's chief aim was to spread the new Russian political model on a global scale. This was one reason for the Russians wanting to infiltrate the British establishment. The other was to find out about the level of British infiltration of Soviet Russia. Events such as the Lockhart Plot had made the Bolshevik regime, still young and vulnerable to instability, fearful of the British, and the Russians wanted to have contacts passing information from within British Intelligence and the Foreign Office.

It would have been very difficult for a Russian to pose as British for any length of time in a high position and to get away with it. Sidney Reilly had managed to work for the British in Russia, but of course he was Russian. British spies such as Paul Dukes had successfully pretended to be Russian during and immediately after the Russian Revolution, when Russia was made up of many different provinces and regions, accents and regional characteristics. The institutions of the British establishment were staffed by well-educated higher-class men and women, and so a Russian posing as British would have been much easier to detect. Recruiting British natives must have seemed the best way forward, the only question being whether these recruits would prove committed in the long term. The Russians would be truly ambitious in the scope and scale of their infiltration, pushing the recruits to achieve extremely high positions within British secret and political life.

The man who began to set up the spy ring later known as the Cambridge Spies was Arnold Deutsch, an Austrian Jew. An academic and former student of the famous sexologist Wilhelm Reich, Deutsch was exactly the type of man needed to appeal to young intellectuals such as Philby, Burgess, Maclean, Blunt and Cairncross, as he understood the new social conscience of young British men of their class and position in society. The Mitrokhin Archive reveals that Deutsch was passionate about change, both politically and socially: 'Deutsch's vision of a new world order included sexual as well as political liberation.'

It was Kim Philby whom he first approached, laying the foundation stone of the Cambridge spy ring.

Of the five men, Guy Burgess was at first the most openly communist. He went on marches and he was at the forefront of the university social scene, much of which was socialist and increasingly communist. Anthony Blunt was cautious and methodical by nature, and it took him some time to believe in the cause. Both Burgess and Blunt were homosexual (Maclean was possibly bisexual) and they mixed in a socialist circle, but it was not exclusively gay (they were both also members of the secret and exclusively elite social society The Apostles). Whilst Donald Maclean developed a social conscience and became more left-wing as his university days passed, little is known about John Cairncross, particularly because he arrived later than the others and was less involved in the social scene.

By October 1932, Philby was coming round slowly, a socialist, but not yet a committed communist. In his memoirs *My Silent War*, he later wrote: 'It was the Labour disaster of 1931 which first set me seriously thinking about possible alternatives to the Labour Party.' Hunger marchers from the north-east of England went through Cambridge en route to London, and Philby was one of the students who marched a short way with them and helped feed them. In 1932–33, Philby was the treasurer of the Cambridge University Socialist Society, his first official declaration of his left-wing views. Meanwhile, Maclean was a member of the British Communist Party and planning to go to Russia as an English teacher after university, and Burgess was firmly committed too, having become a member of the Communist Party under the aegis of the economics lecturer Maurice Dobb. Dobb was a communist who debated in the Cambridge Union, and it has been suggested that he was a talent spotter for the Russians at Cambridge, but there is no unassailable evidence of this, although he *may* have been involved in Philby's own recruitment. Dobb's position as a lecturer gave him a captive audience and communist sympathies were running through Cambridge like a fever.

Talking to the writer and journalist Phillip Knightley in Moscow at the end of his life, Philby explained his feelings at this time: 'I had already decided at nineteen, after a good look around me, that the rich had had it too damned good for damned long and that the poor had had it too damned bad and that it was time that it was changed.' At Christmas 1932, Philby stayed with a mining family in Nottingham. He was trying to see things as they really were, away from the cosy and privileged world of university life. To this end, he also went to other countries on his university holidays, to Hungary, Germany and France.

By the time that he finished his time at Cambridge in June 1933 with a 2:1 in economics (the other four members of the Cambridge Five would achieve first class degrees), Philby had decided to become a communist. He told Phillip Knightley that he went to see Maurice Dobb on his final day at the university and asked the best way to become one (of course, Philby's word is never beyond doubt). Dobb apparently told him that he could give him a contact with an anti-fascist communist group in Paris.

As Knightley has written, this was not the usual route to becoming a communist; the easiest way was to go into the British Communist Party headquarters in Covent Garden, London, and sign up. It is possible that Dobb thought that Philby would be more use to the Comintern outside Britain, but it could also have been a deliberate manoeuvre to place him within the recruiting grasp of the Soviets. Becoming an open member of the Communist Party would have hindered Philby in his task to get into British Intelligence.

After a short time in Paris, Philby was sent by the communist organisation to Vienna. Austria was in a state of turmoil, still reeling from losing its empire in World War One, and there was a great division between Roman Catholicism and secularism. By the time he arrived in Vienna, there was fighting in the streets and communists were under a great threat from the extremely right-wing ruling government. Philby worked as a courier – his British passport gave him great freedom of movement – for the International Workers Relief Organisation and saw real violence in Vienna.

Philby met and began an affair with a young communist, Litzi Friedmann, whom he would soon marry to get her out of Austria and harm's way. They arrived back in London in May 1934, having stopped off in Prague and Paris to meet influential communists. According to KGB files smuggled out by Vasili Mitrokhin, it is likely that it was a friend of Philby's new wife, Edith Suschitsky, who alerted Arnold Deutsch to Philby's potential for Soviet recruitment. This helps explode the popular myth that Philby was an active Russian agent whilst still at Cambridge University, although his contacts there would make up the Cambridge spy ring.

Just as in a spy thriller, Philby and Arnold Deutsch first met on a park bench in Regent's Park in London in June 1934. His first assignment would probably have been to simply write an essay about the problems of the West as he saw them. Then Deutsch would have worked up, instilled and nurtured the seeds of the fear of fascism then rising in Germany, Italy and Spain, and pointed out the dangerous trade links between Britain and Germany. There were many pro-Germans in Britain at this time, especially amongst the upper classes, and this would lead to the desire for the appeasement of Hitler right up to the eve of World War Two.

One can imagine how Deutsch appealed to Philby. Articulate, intellectual and urbane, Deutsch must have seemed worldly and glamorous to the young graduate. He skilfully manipulated the political and social preoccupations of Philby (almost definitely techniques trained by Moscow). Philby never named Deutsch as his recruiter, though the Mitrokhin Archive later confirmed this. However, Philby gave some idea of Deutsch's initial methods in conversation with Phillip Knightley in 1988: 'He told me he appreciated my commitment; the question was how best to use me. I should not go off and die on some foreign battlefield or become a war correspondent for the *Daily Worker*.' Philby went on to say that for two years he was not operational, and that Deutsch was constantly testing his commitment to the cause. But this is slightly disingenuous. Philby was doing things for Deutsch: he was leading him to other possible recruits. The pressure was on Deutsch to deliver. Using Philby as his entry point into the privileged world of Cambridge University, Deutsch asked Philby to provide him with a list of possible fellow recruits, ones with potential for penetration.

The Russians usually set up rings of five, at least they had in other countries until that time. There was no knowing which spy would be able to penetrate to get the information required, and having a ring meant that they could help each other, warning each other if needed, and it is likely that each member of the ring would know little to nothing of the detailed operational activities of his partners. The Cambridge spy ring was recruited to be classic straight penetration agents: having the contacts and disposition to embed themselves in the establishment, their purpose was to dig into the very fabric and infrastructure of British society like moles. Their briefs would be to report back what they read, saw and heard, pass on high-level documents and even influence British security and foreign policy if possible. But there was no knowing if this would work as the Russians had never tried such an operation before with British subjects, as far as we know. The key targets for Russian penetration were the Foreign Office, SIS (Secret Intelligence Service, now MI6, Britain's security in the wider world) and MI5 (domestic security).

Donald Maclean was top of Philby's list. He was already openly a communist, with the immediate ambition of going to Russia to teach English or perhaps study for a PhD. He graduated from Cambridge in June 1934 with a first class honours degree in modern languages, and this would have made him especially attractive to the Foreign Office. Philby sounded out Maclean in August that year, and soon Maclean had changed his mind about his immediate future, deciding to study hard for the rigorous Foreign Office exams.

Although this has since been proven by the release of Russian archives and through investigation, Philby denied it to Phillip Knightley at the end of his life: 'I didn't know about Maclean until after the (Second World) war started, but I doubt that he was recruited at university. So the whole idea of a Cambridge ring or a Cambridge cell just doesn't stand up.' This shows why his memoirs and interviews have to be read with caution. When dealing with 'operational matters', he was knowingly dishonest.

Neither Philby or Maclean ever divulged the content of the conversations which led to this change of direction, but it can be imagined that Philby persuaded him that he could serve the communist cause better by working for the NKVD (the Russian People's Commissariat for Internal Affairs). Incredibly, Maclean's first code name was SIROTA, the Russian for orphan. This unimaginative moniker was of course a reference to the death of his father in 1932. The deep effect that his father's loss had on Maclean was probably a major factor in his recruitment, making him more vulnerable and malleable. Maclean was asked to tell nobody of his recruitment, and after going through Philby he began to have contact with Deutsch.

The irrepressible Guy Burgess was actually at the bottom of Philby's list. Burgess was an unlikely spy, being so extrovert by nature, although this would sometimes work in his favour. Maclean had been given instructions to be less open about his communist allegiance – the Foreign Office would be wary of an open communist. However, Burgess sensed this change in his friend and pestered him about the reason. Maclean eventually told him. From then on, Burgess was also in. Deutsch must have had reservations about Burgess, largely due to his flamboyance and open homosexuality (then of course a crime), but he either saw something in him – he did have a first-rate mind – or felt that it would be safer to have Burgess inside the ring. According to the Mitrokhin Archive, Burgess is reported to have said to Deutsch that he was 'honoured and ready to sacrifice everything for the cause'.

The fourth to be recruited was Anthony Blunt, who wasn't taken on until early 1937. Burgess, Blunt's close friend, set this up. Already a rising art historian, Blunt was fluent in several languages, particularly French, and he was an archetypal Englishman in manner and appearance. Less impulsive than Burgess and seemingly less committed in the beginning than Burgess, Philby and Maclean, Blunt had been less open about his feelings than the others. Blunt's main motivation seems to have been the coming fight against fascism, but his life would have many contradictions that cast doubt on this.

In April that year, the fifth and final member of the ring, John Cairncross, was recruited by James Klugmann, a friend of Maclean who was probably not considered for recruitment himself as he was so notoriously a communist. The pitch to Cairncross was ostensibly to help the Comintern in the fight against fascism. Like Philby, Cairncross first met Arnold Deutsch (known to the spies as 'OTTO') in Regent's Park. Cairncross later wrote in his memoirs *The Enigma Spy* (which also have to be read with care): 'Suddenly there emerged from behind the trees a short, stocky figure aged around forty, whom Klugmann introduced to me as Otto. Klugmann promptly disappeared.' Cairncross would later claim to not know of the existence of the other four as Russian agents, and this could well be true.

The Cambridge Five were now in place. It had taken almost exactly three years to set up the ring. Their Russian and German code names (Deutsch was Austrian) were as follows: Philby: SYNOK/SOHNCHEN (Sonny, on account of his youth); Maclean: SIROTA (Orphan, later HOMER); Burgess: MADCHEN (Little Girl, a reference to his homosexuality); Blunt: TONY (incredibly transparently); Cairncross: MOLIÈRE (his favourite French writer, whom Cairncross would write books about much later). With the ring formed, it was now a matter of positioning. To achieve penetration would take many manoeuvres and in some cases would require burying the past.

The fact that all five men had shown left-wing and communist sympathies when they were young was obviously what had attracted the Russians to them in the first place as potential agents, but this presented its own problem. The institutions into which the agents were instructed to bury themselves would were very wary of any radical tendencies and backgrounds. Vetting procedures were far less rigid than they are now, but any overt show of radicalism not demonstrably recanted would have barred entry to these pillars of Britain's infrastructure. The five now had to distance themselves from their pasts, to varying degrees, and reinvent themselves.

While the five had to make their way on their own and with the help of their not inconsiderable social contacts, they had guidance from Deutsch, his bosses, and later other controllers. Both Philby and Burgess lurched from the far left to the right in their political stance, pretending to have abandoned their earlier leanings. This must have been hard to understand for many of their 'comrades' and Philby later spoke of the discomfort of having to do this, although in his eyes it was for a greater cause.

Through a contact, Philby managed to become the editor of a small and declining literary magazine, *The Review of Reviews*. It was right-wing in outlook and was actually trying to get funding from the Nazis in Germany. Philby made several trips to Berlin and even had an audience with Germany's foreign minister, Ribbentrop. In the end, the Nazis decided to invest in another venture (they wanted to broaden their influence in British cultural life) but Philby had strengthened his right-wing credentials.

Meanwhile, Burgess had gone on a holiday to Moscow in the summer of 1934 with an old school friend. He boasted that as a freelance journalist he had interviewed leading Soviet officials, including

Nikolai Bukharin, but now began to claim this trip had prompted his disillusionment with communism as the reality of post-revolution Russia was austere and far from utopia. The potential that Deutsch had seen in Burgess was beginning to show itself. His social ability and extrovert personality were enabling him to make necessary contacts to reinvent himself. However, he went much further than just disassociating himself from his communist past. He tried to get a job at the Central Office of the Conservative Party; although not successful, he made many useful contacts there.

It was a contact from Cambridge who got Burgess a job. His friend Victor Rothschild of the banking dynasty got him a part-time position as an investment advisor to his mother, despite the fact that Burgess knew next to nothing about financial markets; he hadn't even studied economics, but history! This job paid well and gave Burgess a respectable status, as the Rothschilds were very establishment. This was just the beginning. Burgess also became a member of the Anglo-German Fellowship. This society met regularly in London, usually at the German embassy, and it was a hotbed of Hitler appeasers and admirers, some of them close to power. Many members had dangerous views on racial purity, including anti-Semitism, and their influence would pave the way for the Munich Agreement.

The views expressed at Fellowship meetings were the exact opposite of those held by Burgess, but the whole point of infiltrating was to change his image. On the orders of their Russian controllers, Burgess soon introduced Philby to the Fellowship, and Philby would go on to write some pamphlets for them. In a famous photograph of one of the society's dinners in a huge hall, Philby can just about be made out sitting at one of the tables. Both Burgess and Philby had managed to jump from one end of the political spectrum to another in the space of just over a year. Being among such people as were in the Fellowship, with some very disturbing views, must have strengthened their own views and vindicated their decision to help the Comintern to fight fascism.

While Burgess and Philby were embedding themselves in the British far right, Donald Maclean had gone straight for penetration of one of the institutions to which the Russians directed him. He passed the Civil Service exams. At his interview, he was asked to explain his former communist allegiances, but brushed them aside, saying he was leaving them behind: 'At Cambridge, I was initially favourable to it,' he said, 'but I am little by little getting disenchanted with it.' Maclean was assigned to the Foreign Office. After serving for eleven months in London on the Spanish desk of the League of Nations Department, he was sent to the British embassy in Paris as third secretary.

Anthony Blunt was still a don at Cambridge at this time, publishing many articles on art history and rapidly gaining a reputation in those circles. Like Burgess a year before him, he went on a trip to Moscow with his brother in August 1935; this was a fashionable destination among left-wing thinkers at this time. It wasn't long before Blunt was also lecturing at the elite Courtauld Institute of Art in London. He went to Spain with the poet Louis MacNeice in March 1936; this was more an artistic trip than one directly connected to the Spanish Civil War, but it is likely that what he saw there on the streets helped Blunt make his decision to help the Russians. The threat of fascism posed by General Franco probably hardened Blunt's resolve to help out in some way, as would the death of his communist friend John Cornford in that same war. It was not until 1937 that Blunt was recruited to the Comintern, but he was definitely mixing with socialists and communists throughout the 1930s, as well as helping Maclean penetrate the Foreign Office. Having not joined any openly communist groups or societies, however, he could be perceived as guilty of only mixing in those circles. Blunt would act as a Soviet talent spotter from 1937.

John Cairncross had also not joined any communist organisations, although he had been a member of the Cambridge Modern Languages Society, which had links to the British Communist Party. As the writer Tom Bower noted in his obituary of Cairncross in *The Independent* on 10 October 1995, 'His left-wing sympathies were noticed by

Anthony Blunt. The KGB's talent spotter disliked Cairncross as an unsociable, insipid personality, and the sentiment was reciprocated.' This animosity was not surprising – both men would make many enemies because of their 'difficult' personalities, Blunt mainly because he was distant and aloof, and Cairncross because he was vain and arrogant.

But there is no denying that Cairncross was extremely intelligent. He achieved the top score of his year in the difficult Foreign Office entrance exams by more than a hundred marks. At the Foreign Office Cairncross would meet Donald Maclean and dislike him too; it seems that he liked few people. As mentioned earlier, he later said that he did not know about the other agents, and would not find out until 1951.

It had been decided – with either Deutsch or his boss Alexander Orlov – that Philby should try to break into high-level journalism, and Philby's father used his contacts to get his son an interview. He was taken on as a stringer (piecing together unsolicited stories) by *The Times*, and in February 1937 he arrived in Spain to report on the civil war from the fascist Franco's side (his membership of the Anglo-German Fellowship can only have helped). In July of that year, he became the official correspondent with Franco's forces for *The Times*. This was a very quick rise, but it has been said that Philby was a good journalist, and his later memoirs did show that he had natural writing ability. The Russians had achieved two things by this development. Firstly, they wanted inside information on the Franco war effort (the Russians were supporting the Republican side), and secondly, this posting helped to bury Philby's communist past deeply.

Philby reported to his Soviet contacts (sometimes in England but usually in France) and managed to get very detailed information on the fascist troop movements and weapons capability. In his memoirs, he tells how he was arrested for not having a relevant travel permit and had to swallow some contact codes written on a tiny piece of rice paper. But the most significant event that happened to him in Spain was when the jeep he was travelling in with three other journalists was hit by a Republican shell. The other three were killed, one outright and the other two later in hospital. Philby escaped with head wounds and one to his arm, all treatable. It had been a lucky escape, and General Franco personally decorated him for bravery with the Red Cross of Military Merit in 1938. Philby remained in Spain until July 1939, when he became war correspondent for *The Times* in Arras, France, just before the outbreak of World War Two.

Back in London, Guy Burgess had become the private secretary to a young Conservative Member of Parliament, Robert Macnamara, who was also a member of the Anglo-German Fellowship. The tasks that Burgess dealt with were mainly administrative, but he met a lot of influential people and must have gained a great deal of inside political information, which he undoubtedly passed to his Soviet control. With Macnamara and an admiral who was also an ex-director of Naval Intelligence, Burgess attended the Nazi Nuremberg Rally. Burgess was drinking heavily and leading a rowdy lifestyle by this time: the parties at his London flat in Chester Square were becoming infamous, as was his sometimes inappropriate personality and lack of personal hygiene. Burgess was usually dishevelled (often after a night's drinking), and many contemporaries commented on his nicotine-stained fingers and filthy fingernails, although he seems to have worn good-quality clothes. But his behaviour and appearance could be very deceptive – he had a razor-sharp mind and was constantly gathering information. Stories about Burgess are legion, but his larger-than-life legend could mask his secret activities very effectively.

In 1937, Burgess got a job at the BBC as a producer on a weekly political programme *The Week in Westminster*, where most of the prime movers of the political scene came through the studio. Records released by the BBC in August 2009 show that Burgess was not always on good terms with his bosses. They confirm that he spent most of his time out of the office 'making contacts', and it is probable that these contacts aided his spying as much as his BBC work. Perhaps ironically for a communist, Burgess insisted on travelling first-class on BBC business, claiming this on his expense account, when employees were expected to travel second-class. His argument in a memo to his bosses was, 'I normally travel first-class and see no reason why I should alter my usual practice when on BBC business, particularly when I am in my best clothes.' The records also reveal that Burgess claimed eleven pounds a months in expenses to entertain his 'contacts', the equivalent of twelve hundred pounds a month today. A memo written by a BBC administrative officer on 20 April 1943 (Burgess would work intermittently for the BBC until 1944) reads that his expenses 'are far too high. I realise that a certain amount of drinking at the bar is inevitable, but I cannot believe that it is not possible to do business with responsible MPs except at the bar.'

At the end of 1938, Burgess managed to get himself into the Secret Intelligence Service through contacts. He became a member of Section D (for Destruction), very recently set up to invent ways of sabotage and psychological warfare, to be used in an upcoming war. The Mitrokhin Archive states that the official purpose was to find ways of 'attacking potential enemies by means other than the operations of military force'. This really was a fledgling department, and it was also to be Philby's route into SIS, on the recommendation of Burgess. In June 1940, having been evacuated along with the British forces from France, the journalist Philby was soon working under Burgess at Section D.

Donald Maclean worked at the British embassy in Paris right up to when the Germans were approaching that city in 1940. Dedicated and diligent, he was rising fast and becoming known as a 'career diplomat', already being talked of as a future ambassador. In Paris he met a rich young American, Melinda Marling, and married her. It is almost certain that Maclean was passing anything of value that came across his desk to the Russians; Paris was a key embassy, as it was set to be the centre of Hitler's push through Western Europe. Both he and John Cairncross were able to furnish the Russians with details of developments in the Spanish Civil War and of anti-Soviet feeling in the West.

As already mentioned, Cairncross was with the Foreign Office in London. At the outbreak of World War Two in September 1939, he was given the key position of private secretary to Lord Hankey, overseer of Britain's intelligence services. He later denied that he had had access to early atomic secrets at this time, but it is known that he passed on a large number of secrets concerning military and political affairs. Perhaps most importantly, he was able to tell the Russians that many in the cabinet were still anti-Soviet and wanting to appease Hitler. This of course influenced Soviet thinking; the signing of the Nazi-Soviet Pact in 1939 is the main example.

Having become a Soviet agent in early 1937,

Anthony Blunt was then chiefly used as a talent spotter by the Russians. With his continuing ties at Cambridge University and within the London art world, where many had socialist if not communist leanings, he was in a prime position to pick out any potential recruits. One such was a young American Cambridge student Michael Straight, who had also gone on a trip to Moscow with Blunt and his brother Wilfred in 1935. Blunt now approached Straight on behalf of the Russians and recruited him (Straight will figure later in this story).

At the outbreak of World War Two, Blunt offered himself to military intelligence. He had to undergo a grilling about his Marxist leanings in the past, but he was cleared. Blunt's biographer Miranda Carter discovered that Blunt later saw his MI5 file when he was working for MI5 and that that there was a postcard from the communist don Maurice Dobb in it. In the postcard, Dobb gave his seal of approval about Blunt to a left-wing magazine, recommending Blunt as a writer for it, and details of his 1935 trip to Moscow. Even in those days, when there was no positive vetting as we know it now, the Russians were right to be so assiduous in ensuring that their recruits buried their pasts.

The penetration was now complete, with five of the ring in position. It was now only a matter of how far they could rise.

The signing of the Nazi-Soviet Pact of 23 August 1939, a non-aggression pact between the two powers which stipulated that one would remain neutral if the other was attacked by a third party, should have shaken any ideological commitment felt by the Cambridge Five. Essentially, it meant that the Russians were willing to cooperate with Hitler as a way of gaining time to formulate a plan. Stalin felt that the Nazis would never dare to invade Russia and therefore decided to avoid conflict; the Russians were not yet directly threatened by Hitler, and did not trust Britain anyway. Indeed, partly thanks to the information supplied by Cairncross from the Foreign Office, the Russians knew that there was much anti-Soviet feeling in the British corridors of power and, even at that very late stage, a willingness by many to appease Hitler.

Of course, one of the main reasons for the Cambridge Five to join the Comintern was to fight the menacing spread of fascism in Europe. Now that Russia had committed not to fight the Nazis, they should have felt betrayed. Miranda Carter states that there is witness evidence to suggest that both Blunt and Burgess were confused and angry by the new development, but it did not stop them from continuing to work for the Russians. It is highly probable that the Soviet controllers reassured them that the pact was a temporary tactic to give Stalin time to see which way the wind was going to blow and enable him to make the right choice in the long run.

Stalin was implementing his policy of ridding himself of any dangerous elements (as he saw them) within the Soviet machine. The Great Purges of the middle to late 1930s were still underway. This mixture of purges and change would lead to the deaths of around twenty million Russians, through starvation, murder and the labour camps. Not all of this was known in the West at this time, and Stalin was very good at covering his murderous tracks. But minds as acute as those of the Cambridge Five would surely have heard rumours they would have questioned. There were already some reports coming out of Soviet Russia at this time about brutalities, and intellectuals such as George Orwell had already turned their backs on communism, after seeing this ruthlessness first-hand in the Spanish Civil War.

There was also purging going on much closer to them, although they would not have known it at the time. By 1938, two of Deutsch's immediate bosses, the London illegal residents Teodor Maly and Ignati Reif, had been recalled to Moscow and shot because of Stalin's unfounded paranoia. According to the Mitrokhin Archive, Maly knew his fate before he went to Moscow but decided that he would rather die there, as they would get him in London anyway. And a third, Aleksandr Orlov, defected to the United States just in time, threatening to expose Russian agents if he were apprehended.

Philby was shaken in his commitment for a while after Stalin's signing of the Nazi-Soviet Pact and had no contact with his Soviet control, although they were reconnected when he joined SIS. In his memoirs, written in 1967, he says that despite his confusion he decided 'to stick it out, in the confident faith that the principles of the Revolution would outlive the aberration of individuals, however enormous'. He then goes on to quote a passage from Graham Greene's novel *The Confidential Agent* (Greene had been a colleague in SIS and would later be a friend), which he says sheds light on his own attitude to the cult of Stalin. In the passage, a character's motivations for choosing a side are revealed as a decision that is not regretted and abandoned later; one leader is cynically said to be no better than another in the end, and only history can judge if the decision was the right one.

The 1940s were the key spying years for the Cambridge Five, first during World War Two and then during the Cold War. For most of the war, after the abandonment of the Nazi-Soviet Pact and the Nazi invasion of Russia, the Cambridge spies were spying for an ally. But after 1945, when the Cold War was beginning to freeze divisions between Eastern and Western Europe, Russia was enemy number one to both Britain and the United States. For reasons of space, it is not possible to go into every aspect of the espionage that took place, but an overview of the damage these five men caused – and the help they gave to the Russians – should suffice here. This is important because the Cambridge Five are said to have done more damage than any other spy ring in history.

After starting in Section D of SIS in the summer of 1940 under Guy Burgess, Kim Philby was sent to Hertford for training and was then moved to Special Operations and became a teacher of sabotage and subversion in Hampshire. In the following year, he joined Section V under a Major Cowgill. He was soon made head of the Iberian subsection, covering Spain and Portugal (his knowledge and experiences of Spain would have been invaluable here). His remit was British intelligence gathering in those two countries, and he was based in St Albans, Hertfordshire and then in London. Philby had moved up very quickly, and he worked hard, gaining a reputation for thoroughness and competence. So much so that in 1942 his section was given responsibility for counter-intelligence in North Africa and Italy.

It seems incredible that Philby could win promotion so swiftly, but it must be remembered that it was wartime and Churchill was reorganising everything. Competent and dedicated young recruits had great opportunities to rise fast, and Philby, never forgetting his Russian orders, took full advantage of this state of affairs. In 1944, his first major coup came: he was made the head of a new department, Section IX, set up to fight communism. So Philby led the SIS department whose sole purpose was to combat the very enemy that he was secretly working for. He must have caused immeasurable damage to SIS in this period. The Russians could also plant information for his department to pick up, with Philby's help. Philby was meeting his Soviet contact regularly, using dead letter drops to pass information, and his intelligence was leaving the Soviet embassy in London by diplomatic bag and ciphered messages and being analysed in Moscow.

In 1945, Philby faced his first real threats of exposure. Igor Gouzenko, a Russian cipher clerk at the Soviet embassy in Ottawa, Canada, defected. He informed the British that there was a Soviet spy working at the heart of either MI5 or SIS. The code name was '*ELLI*'. This could have been Philby – although in conversation with the writer Phillip Knightley years later he denied this. This information was assessed at the highest levels of both SIS and MI5, but nothing came of it. However, when Konstantin Volkov, a Soviet diplomat (really an NKVD officer) attached to the Soviet embassy in Istanbul, Turkey, approached the British embassy there saying that he too wanted to defect, the threat to Philby was far more urgent. Volkov wanted safe passage for his wife and himself to Cyprus and a large sum of money. In return, he told the British that he could name three Soviet spies working in Britain: two in the Foreign Office, and one in counter-intelligence. The first two could well have been Maclean and Cairncross, and the latter was obviously Philby.

The details of the deal offered by Volkov were relayed to London, where – unfortunately for Volkov – Philby read them. He managed to persuade his new boss Stewart Menzies that somebody should be sent from London to Istanbul to arrange a deal with Volkov. Menzies agreed and had an agent in mind, but it turned out that this man was afraid of flying and could only go by ship. Philby, who had already warned his Soviet control about Volkov, volunteered to go himself. Menzies agreed. Philby flew out to Istanbul, and was very leisurely about making contact with Volkov. When he did, the Soviet embassy said that nobody of that name worked there. At about this time, a heavily bandaged man was lifted onto a Soviet plane at the airport. It was obviously Volkov, being taken back to Moscow to an inevitable death. Philby had saved himself and perhaps two others from exposure, but it had been close. This incident, like the leak from Gouzenko, would be used as evidence of his guilt later. In 1946, Philby was posted to Istanbul, becoming the head of the Turkish SIS station under diplomatic cover. There were rumours that Philby was being groomed for the top job, as Chief of SIS. Opinions about this possibility are mixed, but he was certainly held in very high regard in the service at that time.

After two years in Istanbul, Philby was given a prestigious new posting, one of the most sensitive and important jobs in SIS. He was to go to Washington, DC, to become SIS liaison man with the CIA and FBI. He took up his new post at the beginning of 1949, much to the delight of the Russians, as this meant that he would have access to both British and American secrets at a crucial time in the Cold War.

Meanwhile, after Section D of SIS was disbanded, Guy Burgess moved into MI5. There, in early 1940, he was involved in the uncovering of the American cipher clerk Tyler Kent, who was working at the American embassy in London. Kent had access to secret ciphered messages between Churchill and Roosevelt, the gist of which suggested that the United States may join in the war against Germany. Being firmly against this, as well as anti-Jewish, he shared these messages with Anna Wolkoff, a fellow member of a secret society the Right Club. From there, they found their way to Italy and then the German intelligence services.

Wolkoff, who knew Burgess through the Anglo-German Fellowship, had no idea that he was working for MI5, thinking that he was still at the BBC, and she confided in him. Burgess reported what he knew to MI5. Some microfilms containing the ciphered messages were being held at a photography studio; the studio was raided, with Burgess present at the raid, and Kent and Wolkoff were arrested. Kent got seven years in prison, but was deported to America at the end of the war; Wolkoff was lucky not to have been hanged for spying for the enemy in wartime, and she got ten years in prison. Burgess was heaped with praise, and he was even invited to the Prime Minister Chamberlain's country house for the weekend.

Churchill was also very grateful to Burgess and gave him a signed copy of his books. Little did Churchill know that Burgess was a Soviet spy.

Burgess, Blunt and several others lived at 5 Bentinck Street (close to Bond Street) in London in the early war years, and the drunken and wild parties there became legendary. Burgess's drinking and rowdy behaviour had come to the attention of a senior official at MI5, Dick White (a future head of both MI5 and SIS), and Burgess was pushed out of the agency in 1942. He went back to the BBC as a producer, but he continued to be attached to the Foreign Office, no doubt aided by his numerous well-placed contacts, so he had kept his hand in. At the end of the war, he became the private secretary to the under-secretary of state at the Foreign Office, Hector McNeil. Burgess had manoeuvred himself back into a favourable position despite his wayward reputation (McNeil was a heavy drinker too, and enjoyed Burgess's company privately, although it is not known whether they were lovers). However, Burgess became too infamous even for McNeil after a while, and he was transferred to the Far Eastern Desk at the Foreign Office in 1948.

In 1950, Burgess rallied to get a promotion to Washington. Probably with the help of Philby, who was already there as the first secretary, he was given the post of second secretary at the British embassy in Washington, arriving in July. As told by E. H. Cookridge, legend has it that before

Burgess left for Washington, a superior in London warned him not to mention race, homosexuality or communism in America. Burgess is said to have replied: 'Are you saying that I can't sleep with Paul Robeson?' The United States was in the midst of the era of McCarthyism, and there was much paranoia about communists; of course, race and homosexuality both caused controversy.

Anthony Blunt also worked for MI5 during most of World War Two. He worked under Guy Liddell, the head of counter-espionage, and had access to a great deal of information. For example, he could report to the Russians on the German secret radio traffic and on the attitudes of neutral countries to both Britain and Germany, so that the Russians could prepare their postwar foreign policy plans. He even had access to the details of the D-Day landings before they happened. At the end of the war, Blunt also undertook two missions to Germany to retrieve letters that could have embarrassed the British royal family. After the war, he left MI5 and returned to teaching at the Courtauld Institute. He stopped passing secrets to the Russians, as he no longer had direct access to them after leaving MI5, but he was of service to others in the Cambridge ring after the war.

John Cairncross was posted to GCHQ (Government Communications Headquarters) at Bletchley Park in 1941. This was a station where intelligence traffic was intercepted and analysed and where codes were deciphered (later it would become famous for the Enigma machine). Cairncross was able to give the Russians details of German capability (especially the Luftwaffe) and order of battle. In February 1943, he passed on copies of the actual intercepted traffic that showed the German offensive planning that would later that year reach boiling point with the battle of Kursk. The Russians were able to make preparatory air strikes against the Germans, and developed a new missile that could penetrate the new thick German tank armour which Cairncross had warned them about. In 1944, Cairncross actually went to work under Philby in Section V of SIS. Here he was able to supply another German order of battle, that of the SS. When the war ended, he started a new job at the Treasury. He maintained in his memoirs *The Enigma Spy* that he had stopped working for the Russians at the end of the war when they were still an ally. But one of his controllers, Yuri Modin, would later say that Cairncross continued to spy at the Treasury, claiming that he even supplied details of the entire structure of NATO before it was formed.

Meanwhile, Donald Maclean had returned to London in 1940 after being evacuated from Paris. Working from the Foreign Office in London, he was able to tell the Russians in September 1941 about the construction of a uranium bomb that was being built by Imperial Chemical Industries and backed by the British government. In the same year, he was almost exposed by the Soviet defector

Walter Krivitsky, who later committed suicide at a Washington hotel (many believe that he was assassinated by the Russians, though there is no firm evidence of this). It is hard to fathom why Maclean was not unmasked then, as FBI files show that Krivitsky had said that the spy was 'a Scotsman of good family, educated at Eton and Oxford [sic], and an idealist who worked for the Russians without payment'.

In 1944, Maclean was posted to the British embassy in Washington (where Philby and Burgess would later be posted) and he would remain there until 1948. He was also the secretary of the Combined Policy Theory on Atomic Development. Although he did not have access to technical data on the atomic bomb, he was able to tell the Russians about American levels of uranium and the progress of the bomb. Maclean also supplied secret correspondence between Churchill and Roosevelt, Churchill and Harry Truman and Clement Attlee and Harry Truman. As well, he was also able to let the Russians know that the Marshall Plan (America's plan to give financial aid to rebuild Europe after the war) was merely to give the US economic dominance in Europe. As a result, the Russians did not sign up to the Marshall Plan. Both the atomic and general intelligence that Maclean passed helped to shape Soviet foreign policy for years to come. At the end of his term in Washington, Maclean was posted to the British embassy in Cairo, Egypt, where he was promoted to head of chancery. But there his drinking and double life began to catch up with him, and he had a breakdown, which included attacking other embassy staff and damaging property. He was recalled to London, given medical leave and then put in charge of the American desk in London.

The Cambridge Five supplied the Russians with thousands of documents each in the 1940s. As the Mitrokhin Archive reveals, at one stage it was said that Cairncross was taking out documents in a suitcase, and on at least one occasion Burgess dropped top secret papers in a public bar. Cairncross alone passed 5,832 documents to the Russians between 1941 and 1945. The damage to British and American intelligence was severe, particularly after 1945, when Russia was no longer an ally. The Russians had buried the seeds of its ring well, and it had produced much fruit. But a storm was about to hit, and there was no way that the agents could continue to operate as before.

Kim Philby quickly settled into his post-war life in Washington, building up good links with the CIA and FBI and becoming part of the diplomatic dinner party circuit. As Philby said himself in his memoirs, his main task was to strengthen the links between SIS and the CIA, as his predecessor had leaned too far towards the FBI. His reputation as a wartime SIS officer garnered him respect from his American counterparts. Besides the material he was able to gather during work hours, he was undoubtedly able to pick up many useful snippets of information for the Russians through private conversations. The 'special relationship' between Britain and the United States set up between Churchill and Roosevelt in the war, was important and sensitive, and Philby had been entrusted with it. But he was soon to make a fatal mistake: he associated himself closely with Guy Burgess, and he would pay for this dearly when the spotlight fell on Burgess.

When Burgess arrived in Washington in July 1950, Philby let him stay in his family home. Philby by now had a second wife, Aileen (married in 1942), and children. Philby may have taken Burgess under his wing to keep an eye on him because of his outrageous behaviour, and this would have caused little damage if it were not for a future turn of events. Burgess was his usual self in Washington, barely able to mask his anti-Americanism, especially in light of his heavy drinking. As Phillip Knightley relays, he even upset the wife of a high-level CIA operative. She had heard that he could draw well (Burgess was a talented caricaturist) and she asked him to draw her. After several requests he did: he drew her with her dress around her ears and her private parts exposed, according to a witness. This took some smoothing over by Philby afterwards. Burgess seemed to be his own worst enemy, or was his rowdy behaviour a sophisticated act to conceal his true activities?

Based in Washington most of the time, Burgess also made some trips across America to give political lectures on behalf of the British government. He was still drinking heavily, even though he probably knew that this was his last chance of a high-level Foreign Office post (his reputation was catching up with him at last). However, it wasn't Burgess who directly created a threat to the Cambridge Five but Donald Maclean, who had recently taken over the American desk in London after recovering from his breakdown.

The FBI had been decoding ciphers as part of the Venona project (the deciphering of radio messages between the Soviet consulate in New York and Moscow), and the FBI special agent in charge of Russian espionage was Robert Lamphere. He and his team, including top cryptographer Meredith Gardner, discovered that between 1944 and 1945, when Maclean had been serving in Washington, a member of the British embassy staff had been sending messages to the Russians. The code name of the sender was HOMER, and the investigation into his identity had begun in 1949. By mid-1950, the possible suspects had been whittled down to just four names, and Maclean was one of them. What worked against him especially was the fact that Lamphere knew that the messages had been sent from New York, where Maclean had visited his wife regularly during those two years. So the precaution that Maclean had taken to send coded messages from New York rather than from where he was based in Washington was helping to single him out.

As always, Philby had access to this information. He knew that HOMER was almost certainly Maclean, and he warned his Soviet control. If Maclean was arrested and interrogated, he could blow the whole ring, especially as he had only recently had a stress-related crisis. Neither Philby nor the Russians were confident that Maclean could withstand interrogation, and even if he managed to not give up anybody else, Philby could be linked to Maclean through Cambridge University and their earlier friendship. Philby and his controllers decided that Guy Burgess was the best person to warn Maclean. This had to be done personally, as Maclean was already under surveillance from MI5. The idea was for Burgess to have himself sent back to London, warn Maclean and tell him that he had to get away. But Philby told Burgess not to escape from Britain with Maclean, as this would implicate Philby too, and possibly Anthony Blunt.

Guy Burgess rose to the occasion. He had been in Washington for about ten months and wanted to return to London anyway, but he knew the urgency of the situation. The best way to be recalled to London was through bad behaviour. He had already raised eyebrows at the British embassy, but now he managed to get three speeding tickets in one day, in different states. He then tried to use diplomatic privilege and had to pay fines. This was all reported back to Washington. Burgess was sent back to London for abuse of his position, and left America on 8 May 1951. Back in London, Burgess met Maclean at the Royal Automobile Club, and this was not so unnatural, as Burgess had just returned from Washington and Maclean was in charge of the American desk in London. Burgess found Maclean very shaken and still not fully recovered from his breakdown. Whatever they discussed, the actions of the following days told the story.

On Friday 25 May 1951 (Maclean's thirty-eighth birthday), Maclean had lunch with friends in Soho, London. Meanwhile, Burgess was rushing around – he had bought two tickets to go to France with another friend for the weekend but called the friend to cancel. It is highly probable that Burgess had received a tip-off from his Soviet control (Blunt's biographer Miranda Carter has suggested that it was Blunt who tipped him off): Maclean was due to be arrested by MI5 and shown the FBI evidence at the beginning of the next week, Monday 28 May. This had increased the urgency still further. After finishing work, Maclean returned to his family home in Tatsfield, where his pregnant wife was waiting (Melinda was due to have a baby in early June). He told his wife that he had invited a colleague, Roger Styles, over for dinner to celebrate his birthday.

The man known as Roger Styles was really Guy

Burgess, and he duly arrived at the house for dinner. Melinda had never met Burgess before and indeed believed that his name was Roger Styles, as she told MI5 later. After dinner, Maclean told his wife that he and Styles had to go to Andover on business. There was an argument, as Maclean had relatives coming for a birthday party the next day. He packed an overnight bag and assured Melinda that he would be back for the party.

Burgess and Maclean left the house at just after 10.15 p.m. Burgess had to drive fast: it was over ninety miles to Southampton. When they got to the quayside, their ship, the *Falaise*, was about to leave. Burgess left the car haphazardly. When a porter called after them about the car, Burgess shouted that they would be back on Monday. They never returned.

The disappearance of Burgess and Maclean was headline news within days and would remain in the media for months. They became known as 'the Missing Diplomats', and their sudden departure left much confusion. But MI5 and the FBI soon realised the worst, and a public statement was eventually forced from them. When Philby heard the news in Washington, he pretended to be very surprised that Maclean had managed to get away from MI5 (indeed the MI5 surveillance officers had been given the weekend off and this carelessness would later embarrass MI5 greatly). He didn't have to pretend about Burgess: he was genuinely shocked when told he was gone too.

It has never been confirmed beyond doubt why Burgess went with Maclean or at least didn't come back from the continent (he might have been expected by the Russians to escort the nervous Maclean to St Malo and then return). It is likely that the Russians forced him to go; he could no longer be of any use to them now, being close to an alcohol-induced breakdown himself, and could have been a future liability. Or perhaps they tricked him, telling him that he could return after a while. Burgess would have known that this wasn't possible. In any case, the two men travelled through Europe and sailed to Russia from the Baltic, no doubt with Russian help.

Philby knew that it was only a matter of time before he was questioned himself, because of his close association with Burgess. The day came soon. Philby received a letter from his superiors at SIS headquarters asking him to return to London. The reason for the letter and not a face-to-face confrontation in Washington may have been so that Philby would try to escape and incriminate himself, as SIS knew that Philby was an extremely skilled operative and would probably not incriminate himself under questioning. In London he was interrogated by MI5. He managed not to incriminate himself further but was asked to resign from SIS because of his association with Burgess. There was also pressure coming from the Americans, particularly from the director of the CIA, General Bedell Smith, and the head of the FBI, J. Edgar Hoover, who was sure of Philby's guilt, as FBI files show. The following year, in November 1952, Philby underwent a 'secret' trial at MI5 headquarters in Mayfair, London. His chief interrogator was MI5's Helenus Milmo, an aggressive and abrasive questioner.

Philby's record of service had been picked over by MI5 in the previous year, and he faced a barrage of questions. However, Philby knew MI5 and SIS interrogation techniques inside out, and he exaggerated his stammer a great deal to break the flow of the questions and to give himself time to think. Although MI5 were sure that Philby was guilty, they could not prove anything in a court of law, as Philby well knew. A different approach was then used: another MI5 interrogator, William Skardon used his usual softly-softly approach, going home with Philby after the interrogation to collect his passport. Philby later said that Skardon was a more dangerous interrogator than Milmo had been, but Skardon also failed to break him. The next three years were lonely ones for Philby, and he had to take a succession of jobs to feed his family, including working as a salesman. There were some in SIS who believed in his innocence, but there was too much of a cloud hanging over him to allow him to return to the service in any capacity.

Philby was back in the news in October 1955.

The government had been forced to produce a white paper (official report) on the case. In the wake of the defection of Burgess and Maclean, there was constant media and public interest in 'the Third Man' – Philby – fuelled further by the 1949 Graham Greene/Carol Reed film of that name which was ironically not about spying, although Greene had worked under Philby at SIS earlier and would become friends with him later. J. Edgar Hoover was allegedly also involved in this, still convinced of Philby's guilt. He was a virulent anti-communist, and one look through the FBI files shows the mindset of the FBI in the 1950s: Burgess and Maclean often called homosexuals, dope smokers and even cross-dressers in reports. Philby undoubtedly raised Hoover's ire (Hoover was notorious for bearing grudges) because of his earlier orders to favour the CIA. According to Phillip Knightley, Hoover placed an allegation in the press that could link only Philby and no one else to the Third Man role. This led a British MP, Marcus Lipton, to ask in the House of Commons if Philby was indeed the Third Man. Because there was no firm evidence against him yet, Prime Minister Harold Macmillan had to deny this and then issued a statement clearing Philby. Indirectly, Hoover had inadvertently let Philby off the hook.

Philby held a press conference at his mother's home, and there is a series of photographs of him grinning with pleasure. In 1956, his name now cleared, he went to work for SIS in Beirut as a field agent – much lower than his previous standing – under cover of being a journalist for *The Observer* and *The Economist*. It is hard to believe that SIS were still employing Philby, but there were many in the service who thought that he was truly innocent and had been persecuted only because of his friendship with Burgess. However, in 1956, Dick White (the man who had pushed Burgess out of MI5) became the head of SIS, and he wanted to nail Philby.

It was only a matter of time. In December 1961 there was a defection. A KGB agent called Anatoliy Golitsyn approached the CIA in Helsinki, and he wanted to come over in return for information he had memorised. Part of that information was conclusive proof that Philby was a Soviet agent. Added to this, a friend of Philby's from many years before, Flora Solomon, approached MI5 in the early 1960s. She told them that Philby had been a communist as late as 1938, just two years before he entered SIS, when he supposed to be right-wing. Solomon said that she had come forward out of conscience, as she saw that Philby was writing for *The Observer* from Beirut. It only remained to be seen what Dick White at SIS would do with this information.

Nicholas Elliott, a former colleague of Philby's in SIS, was sent out to Beirut to confront Philby in January 1963. He told Philby about the new evidence against him from Golitsyn and Solomon, and Philby was shocked. Then he confessed to being a Russian intelligence officer for a long time. He refused to give further details but promised to meet Elliott again. He never did. Instead, Philby must have alerted the Russians. On 23 January 1963 he was due to attend a dinner party but never went. He did not even tell his new wife or children (he had remarried and they were living with him in Beirut). He sailed on a Russian freighter and was in Russia in four days. Philby had finally come in from the cold.

After the disappearance of Burgess and Maclean in 1951, there had also been repercussions for Anthony Blunt and John Cairncross. Blunt had taken MI5 to search Burgess's flat after he vanished and managed to pocket some incriminating letters; Burgess had hoarded letters and sometimes boasted that he could one day use blackmail. But Blunt missed some notes about political matters from 1939. They were unsigned, but the handwriting was soon traced to John Cairncross, who had had access to that information at that time. When Cairncross was questioned, he denied passing any atomic material to the Russians and was allowed to go because of lack of evidence. It is likely that his Soviet controller Yuri Modin coached him to say that he had communist sympathies but that his association with Burgess was no more than a friendship. He was never prosecuted and moved abroad. This has been seen as a government conspiracy to cover up his spying, although he was forced to confess in 1964 by the MI5 interrogator Arthur Martin and publicly exposed by the journalist Barrie Penrose in December 1979, soon after Blunt was exposed. Cairncross lived the rest of his life in the United States, Italy and France, writing critical books on the French writers Molière and Pascal, as well as his memoirs, and he also worked at the United Nations. He always played down his spying – possibly worried that there was still a faint chance of prosecution – and his memoirs are very limited on that topic. His guilt was confirmed in 1990 by the KGB defector Oleg Gordievsky. John Cairncross died in October 1995.

The Russians tried to persuade Blunt to defect, but he refused, saying that he was too much of a bourgeois. The Mitrokhin Archive states that Blunt told his Soviet contact: 'I know perfectly well how your people live, and I can assure you that it would be very hard, almost unbearable, for me to do likewise.' His close association with Burgess made him vulnerable, but he was confident that he could withstand interrogation. And indeed he did. Blunt would survive at least eleven interrogations in the coming months and years, but he was not broken. It was not until 1964 that he was forced to confess after Michael Straight, whom he had recruited for the Russians at Cambridge in the late 1930s, supplied the information that gave Blunt no choice but to own up. Blunt was offered a deal of immunity from MI5 in return for a full confession. By this time he was Sir Anthony Blunt, Surveyor of the Queen's Pictures, the most prestigious artistic advisor in Britain. Blunt was not prosecuted and was allowed to keep his post, although the government, security services and allegedly the Queen knew about his duplicity. Blunt was finally publicly exposed by Margaret Thatcher's government in November 1979 after pressure from the media, which had seen a feeding frenzy of spy exposures after journalists such as Harry Chapman Pincher published books. He was stripped of his knighthood and other trappings, and he died publicly shamed in London in March 1983.

And what happened to the three of the Cambridge Five who had made it to the other side? Within months of Philby's arrival in Russia, in August 1963, Guy Burgess died of liver failure and hardening of the arteries. He was just fifty-two years old. Philby never saw him before his death. When Phillip Knightley spoke to Philby in 1988, the latter was still angry with Burgess for defecting with Maclean. But it may well have been that the Russians had forced Burgess to go. Burgess had been very unhappy in Russia, never learning Russian well and missing his social circle. He drank heavily, had gay lovers that the KGB tolerated and wrote many letters to friends in Britain. Austere Moscow of the 1950s and early 1960s had not been a big enough stage for the larger-than-life Burgess.

Donald Maclean made more of a life for himself. He became a political and economic advisor to a Kremlin think-tank and wrote a book titled *British Foreign Policy since Suez, 1956–68*, which was also published in the West in 1970. He had less contact with Britain than Burgess, but he was interviewed once on BBC radio about his book and became cagey when the interviewer tried to come off that subject. His wife, Melinda, joined him in Moscow and would later leave him for Philby, before returning to her native America. Donald Maclean died of a heart attack in March 1983, aged sixty-nine.

Kim Philby quickly acclimatised to life in Moscow, although he went through a crisis of confidence in his relationship with the KGB for some years when they stopped giving him work. But he was soon back in favour and in the following years received some of the top awards and decorations offered by Russia. He published his memoirs, *My Silent War*, in the West in 1968, largely in response to other books appearing about him (the book was not available in Russia until years later). After having an affair with Melinda Maclean, Philby married a Polish-Russian woman, Rufina. They were very happy together, and they secretly travelled to Eastern Europe and Cuba (Philby could have been arrested or even assassinated by SIS or the CIA outside the Soviet Union, so these travels had to be covert). Philby gave interviews to both Western and Russian journalists towards the end of his life. He was also visited by his ex-SIS colleague Graham Greene several times (Greene had also written the foreword to his memoirs). Philby died of heart disease on 11 May 1988 at the age of seventy-six. He was given a KGB guard of honour at his funeral.

So what motivated the Cambridge Five? All of them had high-flying futures ahead of them, and four of them were from establishment back-grounds; Cairncross was from a less well-placed background, but his intellect and determination enabled him to break through. We have examined the major factors that motivated them politically and socially. But there must have been more personal reasons which led them to take the risks that they did, remembering that spying during wartime carried the death sentence if caught, and post-war spying a lengthy jail sentence.

Let's start with political ideology. In addition to the political circumstances and sociological factors mentioned above, could the Cambridge Five really be termed ideologues? A faith, a belief, a deep commitment of a political or religious nature (suicide bombers are classic examples of the latter) can motivate individuals to espouse a cause over many years or a lifetime, and perhaps to die for it or risk a life sentence in prison if necessary. But the five were young men just graduated from elite universities, with excellent contacts and potential for conventional futures. When they took up the cause of communism, they may have been initially swept along by the fashionable concept of a new way of living, which would have been intensified by the threat of fascism, the Spanish Civil War (where some of their friends were killed) and deep disillusionment with socialist politics in Britain. However, was that enough to make them continue after the Nazi-Soviet Pact, the defeat of fascism, Stalin's purges and the genocide of twenty million?

In an interview with *The Sunday Times* in December 1967, Philby said: 'To betray, you have to first belong. I never belonged. I have followed exactly the same line the whole of my adult life. The fight against fascism and the fight against imperialism were, fundamentally, the same fight.' Could this really have been true, for Philby or the others? Was it to fight against the threat of fascism (as Britain as a whole and its Allies would within a few years) that they committed to the cause? Or was it the want of a better way of life for those less privileged than themselves, offered in their eyes by the communist template?

What is for certain is that the Cambridge spies were not financially motivated, or at least it wasn't their key motivation. The Russians did give them sums of money from time to time: Burgess was often living far above the means of his salary and private income, and according to the memoirs of his Soviet contact Yuri Modin, Cairncross was apparently given a car and money to relocate. On the other hand, Blunt is known to have turned down a pension from the Russians, as his biographer Miranda Carter states. There is no substantive evidence that Philby or Maclean took payment other than for operational needs. In any case, they were hardly being given life-changing amounts of money as other spies have (for example, see Aldrich Ames in Chapter Ten).

Philby was a Marxist ideologue and deeply committed to that system from his university days, and his memoirs from 1967 show that he had not lost faith in this system. His father, St John, was an individual who often went against the grain, which would have made taking a subversive path more psychologically acceptable to Philby. All of the interviews that Philby gave and his own memoirs show him at peace with himself, and he always made reference to the Russians as 'we', but he also comes across as ruthless and firmly committed to the cause. Regarding the agents he had sent to their deaths, Philby told Phillip Knightley: 'There are always casualties in war. Anyway, most of them were pretty nasty pieces of work and quite prepared themselves to kill if necessary.' Philby's memoirs say it all: *My Silent War*. He saw himself as a soldier. Nevertheless, there are those who disagree that he was driven by political idealism. The respected espionage writer Nigel West has commented: 'To this day I am convinced that he was not an ideologue. Spying was just his way of being above lesser mortals.'

Maclean could also be considered a Marxist ideologue. He was an intellectual who thought in concepts and not practicalities, and he had a deep social conscience. Like Philby, the damage he caused to the West was collateral damage in his eyes, and he felt as though he had a higher purpose. The death of his father while he was still at university devastated him and made him much more vulnerable to radicalisation. The fact that he settled well in the Soviet Union shows that he was at one with the Soviet mentality in reality as well as intellectually. However, ideologies can blind, and it is obvious that the terrible atrocities that happened in the Soviet Union under Stalin (and later) were mere blips on both Maclean's and Philby's intellectual radar. Then again, Philby and Maclean would have seen the dropping of the bombs on Hiroshima and Nagasaki, the Korean War and later Vietnam as atrocities too, carried out by the West.

Burgess was caught up in the excitement and may have been committed at the beginning, but not after his defection, when the reality of Soviet life was all around him. He thrived on being the centre of attention, and while he had a brilliant mind and understood political theory well, he did not show the same kind of allegiance to the cause as Philby and Maclean, especially as the years passed. He enjoyed the comforts of the West most out of all of them (with the possible exception of his close friend Blunt), even if he was something of a maverick outsider in terms of his personality and behaviour. Being a homosexual at that time probably already made him feel persecuted, and he was not somebody who liked to live quietly (Blunt was far more repressed about being homosexual). He liked to shock people and delighted in upsetting the status quo, but this was more playfully iconoclastic than genuinely anarchic. However, Burgess must not be considered as just an avuncular roaring boy, as he had a ruthless streak. According to the Mitrokhin Archives, he once asked his Soviet control to assassinate a former friend, Goronwy Rees, who was suspicious of him (his request was denied). Overall, Burgess died a sad man, in sharp contrast to his younger self who had set Cambridge and London alight with his personality.

Blunt was probably committed to the fight against fascism, but he was not a political animal and was out of his depth. Any help he gave the others after 1945 was likely to have been through loyalty to his friends. Blunt also achieved the highest position in British society of the Cambridge Five, knighted and the Queen's personal art expert. The fact that he was also an international authority on art (particularly French and Italian painting and architecture) shows the real Blunt: he thought aesthetically rather than ideologically. Blunt was selfish and aloof, intellectually elitist and very driven about what he truly believed in: art and culture. Politics was not his *raison d'être*, as it was for Philby and Maclean.

Blunt got the brunt of the public's revulsion and outrage, but that was because he stayed to face the music: Philby, Burgess and Maclean escaped to Moscow, while Cairncross lived in America and in Europe. Blunt was not prepared to defect and knew that his spying had largely ended in 1945, when Russia was still technically an ally. (See the end of this chapter, 'Memoirs of Anthony Blunt', for new insights into him, released in 2009.)

Finally, it is possible that Cairncross was driven by a secret hatred of the establishment and the British class system as it stood then (much stronger than it is today), which helps explain his arrogance and insularity. Cairncross also thought of himself as something of an intellectual superman, and he hated the mediocre or average. Added to this was the fact that he had a slight 'chip on his shoulder' regarding his background, surrounded by many other high-flyers who he perhaps felt were intellectually inferior to him, being where they were through contacts rather than merit. Cairncross was on a more personal crusade than the others, fuelled by his own demons. He may have wanted to defeat fascism (as many did), which may have been his early motivation, but perhaps he enjoyed having a secret that nobody else shared, which gave him an inner sense of power that fed his superman self-image.

Added to the general political and social pressures and the individual motivations mentioned above, there was also the skilful manipulation carried out by their Soviet controllers, and especially their recruiter Arnold Deutsch. The Cambridge Five were young and impressionable, and becoming a communist was hardly a stigma at Cambridge University in the 1930s. The Russians played their hand expertly, moulding the five young men into the shape of a ring that was at the centre of twentieth-century espionage, with wide repercussions that changed international relations between Russia and the West, between America and Britain, and inside the Western intelligence agencies themselves.

By the late 1940s, the world was entering a new era. Suddenly, entire cities could be wiped out at the drop of a bomb. It was the atomic age, and every age has its spies.

THE MEMOIRS OF ANTHONY BLUNT

The memoirs of the former Cambridge spy and art historian Anthony Blunt were released to the public on 23 July 2009. As mentioned earlier, Blunt confessed to espionage (the vast majority of which occurred in World War Two) when offered a deal of immunity from MI5 in 1964. He was then allowed to continue in his extremely prestigious role as Surveyor of the Queen's Pictures. However, in 1979, Andrew Boyle's book *The Climate of Treason* focused on 'the fourth man' in the Cambridge spy ring, and despite the use of the pseudonym 'Maurice' (from E. M. Forster's novel about homosexuality of the same name), many knew that the person in question was Blunt.

Blunt knew that he was in danger of public exposure despite the earlier ruling and tried to take legal measures to protect himself. However, in December the matter was taken out of his hands when Prime Minister Margaret Thatcher announced in the House of Commons that Blunt was indeed the fourth man. Blunt was then publicly vilified, forced to make a statement and stripped of his knighthood. He resigned from all his art posts and honorary titles. After making a public statement setting out his reasons and regrets, he became a recluse and a broken man. He began to take refuge in drink, and at the suggestion of a friend started to write his memoirs. On 26 March 1983, Blunt died at the age of seventy-five. His companion John Gaskin entrusted the unfinished memoir to two friends, who deposited it at the British Library with the stipulation that it would not be made public for twenty-five years. Gaskin later moved to Scotland and fell into a deep depression; he threw himself under a train in Dundee in July 1988.

The memoirs run to just over 30,000 words and are mostly in rough typescript with Blunt's corrections present throughout. Some of the pages are in his handwriting, sometimes difficult to decipher. There are no thunderbolt revelations, but this was to be expected – Blunt had nothing to gain from divulging any more than he had confessed to MI5 in 1964. Although they have to be read with caution (after all, Blunt was a spy and a former intelligence officer) they come across as the memoirs of a man honestly trying to explain his motivations and build a picture of the circumstances that had enveloped him. Blunt explicitly states that he did not write his memoirs for certain espionage authors (whom he names), who will probably regard them as 'a compilation of disingenuous misinterpretations and lies'. He says he wrote them for his friends. Even though much of the text is devoted to Blunt's work as an art historian, for which he is still highly respected, the memoirs bring Blunt the spy into sharper focus. Unfortunately for him, his membership in the Cambridge Five always overshadows his vocational achievements in the wider world. And for the purposes of this book, the focus is of course on his espionage activities.

Blunt begins at the very beginning, describing how his mother 'slightly spoiled' him and talking about how growing up in France, surrounded by great paintings and architecture, aroused his artistic and aesthetic interests. When he returned to England at the age of fourteen to go to public school Marlborough College, a tough physical regime and structure and took some getting used to. It was at Marlborough that Blunt showed his first slight rebellion against convention: 'In 1924 John Bowle [later a noted historian], Philip Harding and I founded a paper called "The

Heretick". In it we expressed our disapproval of the Establishment generally and many of its individual manifestations.' The school authorities suppressed *The Heretick* after the second issue.

Blunt says that his friendship with the future poet Louis MacNeice blossomed in their last year at Marlborough, and he describes how they were both very interested in the modernist movement in literature, particularly T. S. Eliot and the early novels of Virginia Woolf. However, he stresses that this interest in modernism, and therefore change, was not carried over into politics. Blunt explains: 'It may seem paradoxical to say so, but this did not imply a political attitude; it was rather a moral judgement; and in fact politics in the strict sense were the one subject which we never discussed, and we were almost completely unconscious of.'

Blunt does concede a streak of controlled rebelliousness in himself and his friends. He adds: 'We were in fact rebels, out to attack the Establishment in all possible ways; but we were rebels within the law, and we were careful enough and clever enough to carry out our crusade without ever infringing the rules of the school.' This shows that Blunt had a healthy youthful questioning of the established order, but was not a radical in the truest sense from an early age. He was not a natural rule-breaker, unlike his fellow Cambridge spy and friend Guy Burgess.

In October 1926 Blunt entered Trinity College at Cambridge University on a scholarship in mathematics, but he would later switch to art history. He writes: 'I did not enjoy my first year as much as I had expected.' The reason was that the life of a new undergraduate was very unstructured, and at Marlborough there had been a strict regime with a structured routine. The lack of a daily timetable seems to have made Blunt feel somewhat lost and unfocused, but in the last term of his second year he was elected to the Apostles, a secret student society. He says that this society was far less revolutionary than it has been often made out to be by the media – but another member was the younger Guy Burgess. Blunt describes Burgess and his own reaction to him: 'It was . . . in the summer of 1931 that I first met Guy Burgess, who had come up to Trinity from Eton in 1930. He could be perverse in argument and in behaviour . . . he would apologise in such an engaging manner that it was difficult to be angry for long.' Burgess's seemingly magnetic and irrepressible personality clearly had an impact on Blunt, after a brief dislike. This is hugely significant, as his friendship with Burgess would influence and change the course of his life.

Blunt explains how the young Burgess had a powerful aura around him and contrasts his personality at Cambridge with the slovenly, promiscuous and outrageous figure he became later. Very personable and one of the best minds in his Cambridge year, 'he was a person of immense charm with a wide circle of friends . . .

his sex life was already fairly full, but he did not blazon it about as he was to do later'. Blunt denies that he ever had a sexual encounter with Burgess, as has been suggested. This is probably true, as Blunt was not Burgess's usual type (Burgess usually went for handsome, athletic men), but it is obvious that they had an intellectual bond. A sexual relationship cannot be ruled out, although Blunt would surely have had little reason to deny this after so many years.

In 1933–34, Blunt took a sabbatical in Rome and travelled extensively in Italy. He writes that it was impossible not to notice the presence of the Nazis allied to Mussolini (Hitler had just taken power in Germany). However, he once again emphasises his political naivety at this time: 'I did not really understand the political implications of what was taking place.' Blunt was preoccupied by art history, but circumstances and monumental political changes in Europe would slowly wake him up to these facts on his return to Cambridge. Blunt: 'I soon found that the grip of Communism had felt even stronger than it had been there . . . particularly strong in Trinity.' He goes on to describe two key communist Cambridge students: James Klugman was 'academically brilliant' and John Cornford was a 'passionate Communist'. The latter would be killed in the Spanish Civil War, and his death would shake Blunt and his friends greatly.

But Blunt was still not convinced by communism himself, although he was beginning to read

Marxist theory by this time: 'At first I was only interested in the affiliation of Marxism to the study of history, in particular to my own field of art history.' It has been known for a long time that Blunt's political awakening was slow, as Philby's had been. But by the end of 1934, Blunt was beginning to understand how Marxism could be applied practically to society. 'I had come to believe – or to think I believed – that Marxism was not only a useful weapon for the study of art history, but that it also supplied the solution to the political problems with which the world was faced in the mid-1930s.' In 1935, Blunt went to Russia with his brother Wilfred. This was his first experience of communism in action, but he stresses that this was principally an artistic trip. (Later in life, Blunt would tell art history colleagues that he was less than impressed with Russian architecture and art. This was probably one of the main reasons why he chose to stay in Britain and face the consequences of his actions, and not defect like Burgess, Maclean and later Philby).

At the outbreak of the Spanish Civil War, Blunt went to Spain with his old school friend MacNeice, by which time he was 'convinced that Communism was the only solution to the world's problems'. This was a key period for Blunt with regard to his decision to work for the Russians, and he tries to explain at length the reasons for his future actions: 'Those who were more politically conscious than myself had, of course, been aware of the problems created by the Wall Street Crash of 1929, and the depression, and unemployment which came after it, and had also foreseen the dangers of Nazism in Germany.'

In contrast, Blunt states that he lived his life in a non-political way, concentrating on his art history studies. The atmosphere was charged with communism and radical thought, but that was not enough to persuade Blunt to act on a political impulse. It was his friends who did that: 'Eventually, however, largely due to the influence of Guy Burgess, but also to the members of the Communist Party mentioned above [James Klugman and John Cornford], I realised that one could no longer stand aside.' The influence of Burgess is paramount here: his persuasion obviously had a huge impact on the politically uncommitted Blunt. It can be imagined how Burgess laid out the reasons why communism was the answer in his passionate and brilliant way, and how Blunt felt compelled to make a stand, as all of his friends were around him. But it should be remembered also that Blunt was older than Burgess and that by this time he was in his late twenties and working as a Cambridge don, so perhaps he should not have been so impressionable.

Once Burgess and others had convinced Blunt that communism was the right way forward, the political upheaval in Europe illustrated to him the necessity of taking a stand: 'The issue of Fascism, as posed to [sic] the advent to power of Hitler, and later by the Spanish Civil War, became so urgent that the Ivory Tower no longer provided an adequate refuge.' This was undoubtedly true for many of Blunt's contemporaries at Cambridge. These were extraordinary times, which led to extreme reactions. 'It became imperative to take sides, and there did not appear to be any question which side one should take. The Chamberlain government was putting up no resistance to Hitler's demands . . . the only force really determined to resist Nazism was Communism, based on Soviet Russia.'

The time was right for the most committed to turn their words into action. Guy Burgess fell into this category; Philby was already under Soviet supervision. 'At a date which I cannot exactly pin down, but which must have been late in 1935 or early in 1936, Guy told me that he had orders to 'go underground'. That is to leave the Communist Party, pretend to have given up his belief in Communism.' This was a major step and the beginning of Burgess's espionage. Burgess also had an eye on his friend: 'At about this time one of my colleagues in Cambridge, Roy Pascal, invited me to join the [Communist] Party. Guy strongly urged me not to . . . and it soon became clear that he had other plans for me . . . he suggested that I should join him in working for the Comintern.'

This tone is prevalent in the memoirs – the

phrase 'he had other plans for me' is very telling. A cynic might say that Blunt was trying to present himself as a waif swept up in circumstances and the pressure brought by Burgess. But all the evidence suggests that Blunt had no firm ideological commitment to communism, other than as a tool to be used against fascism, with the Nazi swastika casting an ominous shadow over Europe. Blunt was an intellectual and not a political animal, as is often the case, and his understanding of Marxist theory was disengaged from the Soviet reality.

Blunt is unequivocal in the memoirs about the gravity of the dilemma before him: 'I was now faced with the most important decision of my life. Looking back it seems easy to say that I should have refused on the grounds that this meant working against my own country.' Blunt says that it was in about 1935–36 that he realised that the fight against fascism was very important – he knew that he had to do something to help. He says that his loyalties were international and not national, and that he might have become a member of the Communist Party. However, it was Guy Burgess, whom Blunt calls 'an extraordinarily persuasive person' who talked him into 'joining him in his work'.

It must be remembered that as Blunt wrote his memoirs he was an ostracised and broken figure, even if he remained outwardly stoical in the glare of the outside world. 'What I did not realise at the time is that I was so naïve politically that I was not justified in committing myself to any political action of this kind . . . the enthusiasm for any anti-fascist activity was so great, that I made the greatest mistake of my life.' He portrays himself as extremely pliable and almost a victim of circumstance.

Blunt admits that he made the wrong choice, something that he avoided in his press conference statement on his exposure in 1979. His lack of remorse in that statement helped whip up the fury against him, but now he was speaking from the heart. Blunt did have a choice – nobody forced him into espionage against his country – but he lays out his political motivation against fascism and stresses the influence of Burgess and others, set against the charged atmosphere in Cambridge. He is also anxious to point out that he does not expect people to understand his choice: 'I am not trying to justify my decision, only to explain how I came to make it, but I would add one note. No one in fact . . . [believed in] the idea of loyalty to one's country as an absolute and universal principle.'

He gets to the heart of the motivations of his generation at Cambridge University, and doubtless many other universities. He tries to justify himself, despite having said that he does not want to do that. This is a man in turmoil, trying to reason with himself and his past, publicly disgraced after moving in the most prominent circles of British society for decades.

But what about Blunt's continued support for the Soviet cause when knowledge of the worst excesses of Stalinism began to filter out? Blunt says that it was not easy to get hold of information about Russia and that much of what was being said about the situation there 'was so grossly distorted that it was easy to dismiss it as capitalist propaganda. We knew of course about the sufferings of the peasants in the collectivization of the farms, but that we regarded as a process which had to be gone through if Socialism was to be created'. He admits that some aspects of Stalin's atrocities did trouble the consciences of his friends and himself: 'We were naturally disturbed by the Russian trials and purges of the Old Bolsheviks in 1935, the generals in 1937.' Later in the memoirs, Blunt confesses that he and Burgess were 'shattered' by news of the Nazi-Soviet Pact.

One of the key topics Blunt discusses is his conscience. He says that it was precisely for that reason that he chose to work for communism: 'I have frequently been accused of hypocrisy for saying that I agreed to work for the Comintern on grounds of conscience, but it is in fact perfectly true.' But yet again he is quick to stress the influence of his Cambridge contemporaries in his decision. Indeed, Blunt does not seem to be able to decide in his mind whether it was a true matter of conscience or the influence of his peers. In truth, it was probably a mixture of both.

In terms of the actual work he did, Blunt

confirms his first role as talent scout for the Comintern. 'My job . . . was to find members of the Communist Party who might be expected to obtain good jobs . . . in which they would have access to information useful to the organization . . . I found three people – one in fact was John Cairncross, whom I did not myself recruit but introduced to Guy.' This is interesting because while Cairncross was known to be guilty in the wake of Burgess and Maclean's defection in 1951 he was allowed to go after MI5 interrogation as there was not enough evidence to convict him. Blunt's explicit naming of him here not only confirms how he was recruited; it also is the first time outside government and secret service circles that Cairncross is confirmed as being the fifth man of the ring. Blunt must have also confirmed Cairncross's treachery in his 1964 interrogations by MI5. It has been said that there was animosity between Blunt and Cairncross, but Blunt denies this: 'It is also untrue to say that I disliked Cairncross, for whom I had great admiration.'

Blunt reveals very little detail about his wartime espionage, his most prolific spying period. He is at pains to show that he was not a hypocrite in taking up the job as Surveyor of the Queen's Pictures, years after his proactive spying is thought to have ended. He emphasises that his connection with the Russians was severed by the time he took up the post, and that Britain had by then proved itself to be 'a bulwark against Fascism and in alliance with others had defeated it'. However, he does acknowledge that although he may not have been actively passing documents or intelligence to the Soviets, the fact that he knew of the continuing activities of three other Cambridge spies and said nothing while working directly for the Queen is damning. He offers no justification of this. It does seem that Blunt rated highly his loyalty to friends. Many would argue that his silence about the others during the Cold War was as heinous a crime as his active spying. Whatever the conclusion, his acceptance of the post of Surveyor of the Queen's Pictures does show both hypocrisy and chutzpah.

Blunt refutes the allegation that he had a hand in Burgess and Maclean's escape and defection: 'It has frequently been said . . . that I played an active part in the arrangements for Donald and Guy to escape. This is in fact not true.' But he adds, vaguely: 'I may have conveyed a message from Guy to his Russian contact but I have no recollection of doing even this.'

Blunt does admit passing a message to Kim Philby in '1955 or 1956' which enabled Philby to re-establish contact with the Soviets after he had to resign from SIS. This is active support for the Soviet cause, but Blunt emphasises that this was simply a sign of loyalty to his old friend, not a reopening of his allegiance to the Russians. 'Why, if I was disillusioned [with Soviet communism] did I pass the message on? The answer is . . .

because Kim was in grave danger and might have to take flight at any moment. This was my last contact with the Russians.'

Regarding his public exposure in 1979, Blunt is honest about how deeply it affected him. 'One solution obviously was suicide, and I thought about it very seriously. Many people will say that would have been the 'honourable' way out. After a great deal of thought I came to the conclusion that it would on the contrary be a cowardly solution.' In handwritten notes at the end of the memoirs, he refutes many of the allegations made against him by the newspapers on his exposure in 1979. He vehemently denies that he caused great damage to Britain by his espionage, or that he sent British agents to their deaths by his treachery.

The memoirs of Anthony Blunt are an insight into the times in which he lived, times of political and social near-chaos. Blunt was swept up in the mood of the epoch, seeing communism as the lesser danger against the ominous darkening of fascism over Europe. He did think about the plight of millions who he felt could be helped greatly by communism, but he was not an ideologue. Rather, the dogmatic persistence and enthusiasm of his friends, particularly Guy Burgess, solidified his views and spurred him to action. But everybody has a choice, and Blunt made his: to betray his country. He shows himself to be a weak man, easily led by those around him, his blind loyalty to his friends continuing even when the Cold War was a real danger to the West. It is a tragic tale, but one of his own making. His spying will always taint him, when his art scholarship should have brought him fame.

CHAPTER 4

KLAUS FUCHS

On 12 October 1949, a man wearing wire-rimmed glasses and a serious expression walked into the Security Office at the Harwell Atomic Research Establishment in Berkshire, England. His name was Klaus Fuchs, a German by birth but by then one of Britain's top nuclear scientists. He had worked extensively on the British Tube Alloys atomic project and the Manhattan Project in the United States. The latter had made it possible for the Americans to drop atomic bombs on the Japanese cities of Nagasaki and Hiroshima in August 1945. These nuclear attacks caused the apocalyptic destruction of the two cities and enormous loss of life, forcing the Japanese to finally surrender in the war with America that had begun with Pearl Harbour. Fuchs was now the acting deputy chief scientific officer and the head of the Theoretical Physics Division at Harwell.

Fuchs approached security officer Henry Arnold, who was affiliated with MI5, and told him that there was something troubling him. Arnold was a friend too, and listened as a friend would, but his professional interest was aroused. Fuchs told Arnold that his father – an academic – was about to take up a professorship in theology at the University of Leipzig in East Germany (then under communist control) and was about to move there from Frankfurt in West Germany. A scientist of Fuchs's standing dealing with atomic secrets needed the highest security clearances, and Fuchs was worried that his father's move to Leipzig could compromise him. Arnold listened as Fuchs asked if he should resign and after a while said, 'If the Russians approached you to give them secrets and put pressure on you, would you give them over?' Fuchs replied, 'I don't know'. Fuchs left the office that day with Arnold promising to think about his predicament. But Arnold did more than that – he told MI5.

It was not until 21 December that MI5 sent one of their top interrogators, William Skardon, to interview Fuchs. Skardon would later interrogate Kim Philby (see Chapter Three), and his technique was to make the subject feel at ease, lolling him or her into a false sense of relaxation. When he judged that the time was right, Skardon would go in for his prey.

It was not just the issue of Fuchs's father that had alerted MI5 and Skardon to a potential security risk. Information had come from the FBI through the Venona Project that suggested a high-level leak within the British scientific community related to atomic research. The decrypted report of coded radio traffic from the Soviet Consulate in New York to Moscow in 1944–45, which is in the FBI files on the Venona Project, is headed: 'MEETING BETWEEN "GUS" AND "REST"; WORK ON ENORMOUS'. It was sent on 9 February 1944 and addressed to VIKTOR in Moscow.

The FBI worked out that 'REST' was the British scientist passing information, but there were four British scientists working on the Manhattan Project in New York at that time, before it was moved to the atomic research and development site at Los Alamos, New Mexico. The four suspects were Christopher Frank Kearton, Tony Skyrme, Rudolf Peierls (Fuchs's immediate superior) and Klaus Fuchs himself. (The scientists had all left the US by 1949 (Fuchs in 1946), so the FBI simply passed this information on and MI5 had to pinpoint the leak.

During their first meeting, Skardon calmly told Fuchs that he was suspected of spying for the Soviet Union. 'I don't think so,' said Fuchs. 'I don't understand . . . I have not done any such thing.' Skardon wrote the following conclusions to his report, to be found in MI5's files: 'I find it extremely difficult to give a conclusive view on the guilt or innocence of Fuchs. His demeanour during our interview could have been indicative of either condition. If he is innocent it is surprising that he should receive allegations of this kind so coolly.' However, Skardon went on to write that Fuchs could be 'a spy of old standing' and ready for an interrogation, and he was confident that Fuchs was the right man to target.

There were to be many more meetings between Skardon and Fuchs. Skardon was gently working on him, gaining his confidence, and occasionally setting little traps for him. On 30 December and 10 January 1950, Fuchs held firm that he was innocent. But on 13 January, over lunch in the town of Abingdon (Skardon relaxed his prey well), Fuchs finally admitted to Skardon that he had passed secrets to the Russians about the atomic bomb. They would meet five more times to go after details, but Fuchs would not give Skardon technical details about the atomic programme, as he felt that Skardon did not have the right security clearance. On 27 January in the War Office, Fuchs gave a detailed technical confession to Michael Perrin, the deputy controller for atomic energy policy, whom Fuchs had known for eight years. Fuchs was still allowed to return to Harwell, but he was under surveillance. After another meeting three days later, he was finally charged with spying under the Official Secrets Act of 1911.

Klaus Fuchs was thirty-eight years old when he was charged with treason. His life had been a very eventful one, and the best source regarding his past is the lengthy statement he gave to Skardon over the course of their meetings, signed on 27 January 1950. These facts were checked and double-checked by MI5.

★   ★   ★

Fuchs was born on 29 December 1911 in Rüsselsheim, Germany. His father was a parson but had political inclinations. Fuchs told Skardon that his father 'always did what he believed to be the right thing to do and he always told us that we had to go our own way even if he disagreed. He himself had many fights because he did what his conscience decreed' – such as joining the Social Democratic Party early on.

This individuality of thinking likely influenced Fuchs. Fuchs said that he had a happy childhood, but he did not have much interest in politics at school, apart from a rebellious period when he wore a Weimar republic badge at a time when everybody else was wearing Imperial badges. Fuchs's badge was torn off. He went on to study at the University of Leipzig (where his father would be offered a teaching position years later) and joined the Social Democratic Party (SPD), helping to organise the student wing of the party. He then studied at Kiel University, where he was passionate about stopping Hitler from being elected and joined the Communist Party to that end, although he continued to be a member of an organisation that had some SPD members. He became deeply involved in student communist politics at the time when the Nazi wing was growing in strength within the SPD, and his life was threatened on one occasion. When Hindenburg made Hitler the Reich chancellor, Fuchs knew that he had to continue his struggle against the Nazis covertly: 'After the burning of the Reichstag I had to go underground . . . I knew that the underground struggle had started. I took the badge of the hammer and sickle from my lapel which I had carried until that time.' The hammer and sickle emblem represented the socialist and communist struggle. Soon after, in 1933, Fuchs fled to France because of the dangers to communists in Nazi Germany.

He always intended to return to Germany. He said in his statement that he believed that a communist revolution would be brought about in Germany, and when that happened 'people would be required with technical knowledge to take part in the building of Communist Germany'. Fuchs now was a naturally gifted physicist, and so he counted himself as one of those people. Like the Cambridge Five, he did have doubts about Russia when it signed the Nazi-Soviet Pact in 1939, but 'in the end I had to accept that Russia had done it to gain time'.

In France, Fuchs was interned as an alien when the Germans began their attack. After his release, he managed to go to England through a family contact and took his PhD in physics at Bristol University in 1937. An academic paper he wrote on quantum mechanics had been published in 1936 and got him a teaching position at the University of Edinburgh. He also gained his DSc there, studying under Max Born. But when Britain entered World War Two, Fuchs was interned again, on the Isle of Man, and then in Quebec, Canada, between June and December 1940. Professor Max Born put in a word for Fuchs, and he was soon back at Edinburgh University. He was then head-hunted by Professor Rudolf Peierls of the University of Birmingham to work on the Tube Alloys programme, the British atomic research project financed jointly by the government and the Imperial Chemicals Company. To do this job, Fuchs had to sign the Official Secrets Act, and he was given British citizenship in 1942.

Not long after starting work on the project, Fuchs made contact with the Russians: 'When I learned about the purpose of the work I decided to inform Russia and I established contact through another member of the Communist Party. Since that time [up to 1949–50] I have had continuous contact.' Fuchs's first Soviet contacts was Ruth Werner, a German communist like him, with the code name SONIA (Fuchs's code name, as mentioned above, was REST). Later, his contact's code name was GUS (perhaps the Russian Alexander Feklisov). In his statement, Fuchs went on to say that he had had to put his mind into two compartments, one for his everyday friend-ships with colleagues and the other for his spying, and that his Marxist philosophy allowed him to do this.

Towards the end of 1943, both Peierls and Fuchs were transferred to Columbia University in New York to work on the Manhattan Project, the

American atomic bomb programme, where Fuchs focused on the problems of gaseous diffusion. In Britain, Fuchs had been run by the GRU (Soviet Military Intelligence) but in the United States he was run by the NKGB (Soviet Security and Intelligence Service). In August 1944, he and other British scientists were moved once again to the Theoretical Physics Division at Los Alamos, New Mexico, headed by Hans Bethe. Fuchs specialised in working out how to implode the fissionable core of the plutonium bomb. His close colleagues at Los Alamos later said that he was amiable and pleasant, taking part in dances and parties in the evenings, but difficult to get to know. He never opened up, which was probably partly a result of his natural intellectual temperament and partly the detachment of a spy. An interesting point to note is that although most of the American scientists had cars, most of the British scientists could not afford them, apart from Peierls and Fuchs. The former had a higher position, but with regard to Fuchs, this does raise the question of whether the Russians were paying him. This has never been established.

The people chosen for the Manhattan Project were the very best scientists from the United States and Britain, including some immigrants, and Fuchs was certainly excellent at his job. He invented techniques for the calculation of the energy required for fissile assembly (crucial in nuclear physics), and one of the methods he co-authored, the

Fuchs-Nordheim method, is still used today. His expertise makes it all the more frightening to think what he could have passed to the Russians. In 1948 the FBI discovered that the leak at Los Alamos had given the Soviets a top-secret scientific report on the gaseous diffusion method of producing uranium 235. Fuchs had specialised in this area in New York, which greatly helped the FBI to narrow the suspects down from four to one.

Fuchs left Los Alamos on 15 June 1946 and returned to England. It was during the first few years after the war that he began to question his allegiance to the Russians and a statement he gave in his MI5 file supports this. But Fuchs did continue to spy for the Russians after the end of World War Two, when fascism had been defeated. He still believed that the Russians would build a new global order, a new way of living. Between the end of 1947 and May 1949, he gave the Russians the theoretical physics to build a hydrogen bomb, which he was then working on at the Harwell Atomic Research Establishment. He also passed over plutonium and uranium bomb test results, as well as the rate of production of uranium 235 in the United States (crucial to building atomic bombs).

It was his father's influence that finally began to crack Fuchs's resolve regarding his position at Harwell. His father also believed that the Russians would build a new global order (this explains why his father was prepared to move to East Germany, under Soviet control). Fuchs did not feel that he could ask his father to turn down the job offer so that he could keep his own, especially since the two of them shared the same hopes and dreams. It was because of this turmoil in his mind that Fuchs had approached Henry Arnold: 'I invoked an outside influence by informing security that my father was going to the Eastern Zone. A few months passed and I became more and more convinced that I had to leave Harwell.' It was then that MI5 seized the opportunity and sent Skardon to work on Fuchs.

The initial court hearing on Fuchs was held on 10 February 1950. The Crown prosecutor said that only three witnesses would be called for the prosecution: William Skardon, Michael Perrin and Henry Arnold. The trial began on 1 March 1950 and lasted less than an hour and a half. The following day Fuchs was sentenced to fourteen years in prison. The Russians immediately issued a statement denying that he had been a Soviet agent. He was lucky, as in the years following the Cold War Russia was still technically an ally (if not in the hearts and minds of many) and so he did not face a death sentence or a much longer prison sentence. In December 1950 Fuchs's British citizenship was revoked. After serving nine years and four months at Wakefield Prison in Yorkshire, he was released on 23 June 1959. He immediately moved to Dresden in East Germany.

In 1959, Fuchs married a fellow communist he had known in his early years in Germany before escaping to France and Britain. He continued to work as a scientist and is credited with helping the Chinese build their first H-bomb. Fuchs became the deputy director of the Institute of Nuclear Research in Rossendorf and achieved widespread professional respect before retiring in 1979. The Russians also awarded him the prestigious honours of the Order of Karl Marx and the Fatherland's Order of Merit. Fuchs died on 28 January 1988, at the age of seventy-six.

What motivated Klaus Fuchs? What led him to betray the country that had taken him in when he was in flight from Nazi Germany? After a period of wartime alien internment, he was given incredible opportunities to further his scientific career in Britain and the United States, and he certainly made a considerable contribution to British and American atomic progress at Harwell and in New York and Los Alamos on the Manhattan Project. Yet, at the same time, he was covertly servicing the Soviet Union. What made Fuchs bite the hand that fed him?

Fuchs was undoubtedly motivated by ideology, perhaps in its purest form. A communist as a youth, he was driven by the fear of Nazism in his native Germany. He was heavily influenced by his father, who was a theologian and an ideologue – and, according to Fuchs, a man of the highest integrity. Fuchs said in his MI5 statement that he and his father were both of the same mindset: they both saw Marxism (rather than communism) as the best chance of a new global order, a new society forged by revolution on the Russian model. Fuchs was an intellectual in the classic sense: he thought in theories, ideas and concepts, not just in physics but also in politics. Fuchs had a high-powered mind, but his ideology was simple and clear to him; the difficult part was bringing it into reality. He decided that the best way was to help the Russians in any way he could, in his case scientifically. Of course, in 1941–42, Russia was still an ally in the war against Hitler. Fuchs may have been incensed that important information he was using in atomic research was not available to an ally, as Russia faced a severe threat from Hitler.

But Fuchs had a conscience. The Nazi-Soviet Pact of 1939 unsettled him temporarily, and he questioned the Soviet foreign policy after World War Two. He also felt guilty about his betrayal of his colleagues at Harwell, and the effect on their work after his exposure. In his mind, he was focused on the new system that the Russians could one day bring about, but as this seemed less likely to be achieved in the short term after the war his doubts multiplied.

Nevertheless, he continued to give information to the Russians as late as 1948 or 1949. This is an indication of either the real depth of his commitment or the Soviet pressure for him to continue. The Russians may have manipulated him at this stage. In any case, by this time he went to Henry Arnold at Harwell to unburden himself, he was clearly in turmoil.

In the KGB archives, there is a short essay that Kim Philby wrote entitled 'Should Agents Confess?' It was written to help KGB officers in their training. In it, Philby analyses the cases of Klaus Fuchs and Allan Nunn May (code name ALEK), who had worked at the Atomic Research Centre in Ontario, Canada, and was sentence to ten years in prison for passing information to the Russians. Philby concludes that neither should have confessed, as there was only circumstantial evidence against them. He says that the MI5 interrogator William Skardon worked on Fuchs's 'tangled emotions'. This is undoubtedly true: Skardon's soft approach led to Fuchs breaking because he was confused. His ideology may have been intact deep down, but he was feeling guilt because of his father and the damage he was doing to his colleagues. Of course, Philby himself managed to stand up to Skardon during their interrogations. Philby was an ideologue, like Fuchs, but perhaps one with more personal vanity. Philby was a professional spy; Fuchs was a professional scientist who spied for the Russians.

So how much damage did Klaus Fuchs cause the United States and Britain by passing atomic secrets to the Russians? The Atomic Energy Commission in the US (which Donald Maclean had been attached to in Washington) spent a great deal of time assessing what Fuchs had actually handed over. His early work on the atomic programme, including a design he patented in 1946, is still top secret, so it is difficult for anybody who does not have access to this information to fully gauge the harm caused to the West and the benefit to the Soviets. Plus, Fuchs was not the first atomic spy to give secrets to the Russians and be caught; Allan Nunn May, mentioned above, was another.

The production of an atomic bomb relies heavily on the production of uranium and plutonium, and therefore no matter how much technical information Fuchs gave the Russians on how to build a bomb, the raw materials needed would have dictated their progress more than anything. Of course, Fuchs also gave information about the US production rates of uranium and plutonium, and this supplied the Russians with valuable guidelines on how many atomic bombs the Americans could produce. The strength of an opponent is all-important in power politics. In 1948 the Russians knew that the United States was not ready for a full-scale nuclear war, which meant they had time to develop their own programme.

The information provided by Fuchs must have helped, but it was probably not indispensable. The head of Soviet atomic development was Laventry Beria, a key lieutenant of Stalin (interestingly, it has been alleged that Beria poisoned Stalin in

1953). Beria did not take technical data at face value, but used it to confirm the findings of Russian atomic scientists. The information passed by Fuchs probably acted as a catalyst and a measurement of Soviet atomic progress, rather than giving them everything they required. It is also possible that Fuchs's data confused the Russian scientists in some ways, as the design for the first American plutonium bomb ('Fat Man') was ordered to be the template for the first Russian bomb ('Joe 1') by Stalin. So the design that Fuchs gave the Soviet Union was sometimes at odds with its own findings, as the Russian development programme had progressed independently with different findings from American development. The data about the hydrogen or H-bomb that Fuchs gave them was also probably not enough alone for them to develop one. The design used was not finalised until 1951, and Fuchs last had access to details about the H-bomb in 1946.

The diplomatic repercussions of Fuchs's atomic spying, confession, trial and subsequent publicity were huge. In 1950, the British, American and Canadian governments were in crucial discussions to decide the future direction of defence plans, and atomic capability was a major thread of these talks. The exposure of Fuchs's spying could not have come at a worse time, and diplomatic efforts were unsuccessful in that year. In fact, diplomatic atomic relations between these three allies would remain strained for several years to come. The

Senate hearings on Soviet espionage stated that Fuchs had caused 'greater damage than any other spy, not only in the history of the United States, but in the history of nations'. This is perhaps a slight overestimation, but when one considers the state of relations between the East and West in the early years of the Cold War, the threat of atomic information leakage was truly venal in the eyes of Western powers. The possibility of an atomic war was real after the dropping of the bombs on Hiroshima and Nagasaki, and the stakes had never been higher. Fuchs had raised paranoia to new levels with his activities.

In 1950, the United States was gripped by McCarthyism. Anti-Soviet feeling was running high, nowhere more so than in the FBI under its director, J. Edgar Hoover. But whilst McCarthyism became a shameful witch-hunt, the Fuchs case added power to the maelstrom: perhaps there really were 'Reds under the bed'. At his trial, Fuchs had given additional information about his contacts, and this would cause massive vibrations across the United States. Fuchs told the court about his courier Harry Gold (code name RAYMOND), who was arrested on 22 May 1950. There was a domino effect, and soon a whole communist ring was uncovered – one of the most infamous cases in the history of espionage.

CHAPTER 5

JULIUS AND ETHEL ROSENBERG

19 July 1953
Sing Sing Correctional Facility, Ossining,
New York, United States
8:02 p.m.
Julius Rosenberg, a thirty-five-year-old man of medium height, was led to the electric chair just as the sun was starting to go down. The first series of electrocutions that swept through his body killed him.

8:08 p.m.
Ethel Rosenberg, the thirty-seven-year-old wife of Julius, was strapped into the electric chair. The first set of currents flowed through her body, but when her straps were undone to check that she was dead, it was found that her heart was still beating. She was strapped into the chair again, and another set of shocks applied. Her heart continued to beat. A third series was applied. Eyewitnesses later reported that smoke rose from her head. Ethel was finally dead.

That very morning, Ethel had written a final letter to her children, Robert, aged six, and Michael, aged ten. The letters were published later that year, as the executions and the legal wrangles leading up to them had caused great controversy. The final letter read: 'Only this morning it looked like we might be together again after all. Now that this cannot be, I want so much for you to know all that I have come to know. Unfortunately I may write only a few simple words; the rest your own lives must teach you.' Ethel goes on to proclaim their innocence to her children.

Julius Rosenberg and Ethel Greenglass were both born into poverty to traditional Jewish families in New York. Ethel was born on 28 September 1915, and Julius on 12 May 1918. Both of them were sickly children, and largely for this reason Julius's mother doted on him. At the age of four, Julius had run into a taxi and was rushed to hospital. His injuries were not serious, but the shock of the accident caused his mother to miscarry her sixth child (Julius was the youngest of five). Julius was a dreamer as a boy and would sometimes sit for hours peering out of a window with his deep blue eyes. He was also said to be very gullible and inno-cent. Ethel also had dreams for her future as she grew into a young woman, but she was more grounded and confident.

As Julius grew older, his father was somewhat disappointed with him; he wanted him to study to be a rabbi, but Julius was withdrawn, bookish, and not interested in that path. He went to the moderately religious Seward Park High School in New York and showed an aptitude for science and mathematics. He then enrolled at the City College of New York to study electrical engineering.

From a young age, Ethel had aspirations to be a singer and actress to escape her poor background. These heady dreams led to friction with her mother, who was not supportive of her artistic ambitions. But Ethel had grown into a headstrong young woman, and she rebelled against her mother all the more. She did perform in small theatres, but the harsh reality of life would eventually force her to take a job as a secretary at the National New York Shipping & Packing Company.

Early on at the City College of New York, Julius became politicised and joined the Young Communist League of America in 1936 (as in Britain, this political direction was very common amongst young people in the 1930s). He was becoming increasingly anti-fascist as he saw Hitler's treatment of his fellow Jews. He read *Mein Kampf* (published in 1926), in which Hitler had laid out his extreme anti-Jewish views, and like many others at the time he saw that fascism had designs on global domination. Julius had previously joined the Federation of Architects, Engineers, Chemists and Technicians, which had strong links to the Communist Party and the American Students Union. But it was at the Young Communist League that he would meet his future wife.

Ethel had joined the league because she had become more and more interested in social justice and economic equality. She wanted to improve the lives of the majority, and communism seemed to promise that it would. She had become involved in union activities, and in August 1935, at the age of nineteen, she led a hundred and fifty female co-workers at the New York Shipping & Packing Company on a walkout. Their actions earned them better pay and conditions, but Ethel was summarily sacked.

Julius and Ethel were married in 1939. Julius graduated in the same year with a degree in electrical engineering, and in 1940 he entered the Army Signal Corps, specialising in radar equipment.

There is some dispute as to when Julius made his first contact with NKVD. The man who was later his NKVD contact, Alexander Feklisov, said that Julius was recruited in 1942. A senior member of the American Communist Party apparently introduced Julius to Semyon Semenov, a NKVD recruiter. At this time, Russia was still officially an ally of the United States, even though there were deep suspicions about the real motivations between both countries, and they kept their secret projects from each other. Feklisov later said in his 2001 book *The Man Behind the Rosenbergs* that Julius gave the Russians 'thousands' of top secret reports, many of them technical, including the design for the armament that the Russians later used to shoot down the U-2 spy plane flown by Gary Powers in 1960, which caused a major diplomatic incident. A design for the cutting-edge Lockheed P-80 was also handed over, not by Julius himself but by one of the American citizens that he helped the NKVD to recruit. But it was when the NKVD discovered that Julius's brother-in-law, David Greenglass, was working on the Manhattan Project that the activities which ultimately led to the executions of Julius and Ethel began.

Ethel's brother David, seven years her junior, was employed as a machinist/technician at the Los Alamos Atomic Research facility, where the bulk of the research of the Manhattan Project was taking place, and where the German-British scientist Klaus Fuchs was spying for the Russians (see Chapter Four). The key charges levelled against Julius and Ethel by the US government later were the following:

1) In 1944, Julius and Ethel persuaded her brother David and his wife Ruth to spy for the Russians and pass over atomic secrets to them.

2) Julius recruited two former college friends, Max Elitcher and Morton Sobell, to spy for the Russians, although not on atomic secrets.

3) At some point between 1946 and 1949, Julius told David Greenglass of his other spying activities, so he was consciously and provably aware that what he was doing was espionage.

4) Julius arranged with the New York Soviet vice consul for a man named Harry Gold to travel to Albuquerque, New Mexico, in 1945 to collect the atomic secrets from David and Ruth Greenglass.

It was the third charge, combined with the arrest of Klaus Fuchs in 1951 (see Chapter Four) which led to this atomic spy ring unravelling. At his trial, Fuchs pointed the finger at Harry Gold.

Harry Gold's real surname was Golodnitsky, and he was born to Russian parents in Berne, Switzerland, on 12 December 1910 (making him thirty-four years old when he acted as a courier for the Greenglasses). When he was four, his parents emigrated to the US. After graduating from high school in 1929, Gold began a career as a chemist. Between 1930 and 1946, he worked for the Pennsylvania Sugar Company (apart from being briefly laid off in the Depression in 1932 and several periods of study which earned him a degree in chemical engineering). The Russians recruited Gold much earlier than Julius Rosenberg, in 1935. In late 1940, Semyon Semenov, the man behind Julius' recruitment, activated Gold as a Soviet operative. From that point until his arrest on 23 May 1950, Gold operated under the code name GUS and chiefly acted as a courier for the Soviets, passing on the intelligence gathered on their behalf.

After Gold was arrested, he admitted to working for the Russians and gave the FBI the name of David Greenglass, for whom he had been a courier. The following year, Gold was sentenced to thirty years in prison, but J. Edgar Hoover, the director of the FBI since the early 1930s and a master of propaganda, portrayed him as a victim of the Russians, probably because he cooperated and exposed Greenglass and therefore the Rosenbergs. In his 1958 book *Masters of Deceit*, Hoover wrote about Gold: 'In promoting the Red cause, he had been almost morbidly self-sacrificed. Denying himself luxuries, spending hard-earned money, wasting vacation periods, making long trips . . . he gave everything he had, including his honor.' Gold was released from prison in 1965 and died in 1972.

Once Gold had named David Greenglass, the former Los Alamos technician and army sergeant was arrested on 15 June 1950. At first he denied that his sister Ethel and her husband had been involved in his recruitment by the Russians. Julius was questioned by the FBI as a close associate but was released the same day. However, over the following weeks, as Greenglass realised the gravity of the situation for himself and his own family, he gave the information that would eventually lead to his sister and brother-in-law's execution. He said that Ethel had been persuaded by his brother-in-law, Julius, to recruit his help on behalf of the Russians, and also that he had seen her typing up information for the Russians. In an interview in July 2001 with *The New York Times* Greenglass denied seeing Ethel type those notes and explained that he had implicated his sister falsely to save himself and his wife. He said that the prosecution had cleverly manipulated him to do so, but that he had had no idea that his sister and brother-in-law would face the death penalty.

Julius was arrested on 17 July, the charges being that he had conspired to commit espionage with Greenglass and Gold in 1944–45. Ethel was arrested on the same charges on 11 August. The author Phillip Knightley has written that Kim Philby may have had a hand in the Rosenbergs' arrest, as scapegoats to shield more valuable Soviet agents, but there is no definite proof of this.

It is important here to understand the political climate in the United States at that time. Senator McCarthy was in the throes of his anti-communist witch-hunt, and the House of Un-American Activities Committee (HUAC) had just a few years before sat in judgement on anybody who had shown communist or even socialist leanings. It was not only those in political and technical positions who were scrutinised – Hollywood was a major target, with screenwriters being blacklisted and their careers wrecked for years, some even being imprisoned for refusing to testify against others. J. Edgar Hoover, among others, was a staunch supporter of McCarthyism, and his all-powerful hold over the FBI certainly did the Rosenbergs no favours.

Throughout the FBI interrogation, Julius and Ethel Rosenberg continued to deny that they were spies. Their trial began on 6 March 1951 at 10.30 a.m. at the United States District Court, Southern District of New York. Morton Sobell had also been arrested and accused of conspiring with the Rosenbergs, and he was tried at the same time. The case was heard before Judge Hon. Irving R. Kaufman and a jury. Leading the prosecution was US Attorney Irving H. Saypol. Emanuel H. Bloch represented Julius while Alexander Bloch defended Ethel. The principal witnesses were David and Ruth Greenglass, Julius' former college friend Max Elitcher, Harry Gold and Elizabeth Bentley (a communist sympathiser who was disgruntled at being excluded from active duty by the Soviets due to her lack of discretion). On 29 March, both the Rosenbergs and Morton Sobell were found guilty. On 5 April 1951, Julius and Ethel Rosenberg were sentenced to death in the electric chair, with their execution date set for 21 May.

Judge Kaufman's statement on sentencing was very powerful: 'Citizens of this country who betray their fellow countrymen can be under none of the delusions about the benignity of Soviet power that they might have been prior to World War Two. The nature of Russian terrorism is now self-evident . . .' The judge went on to say that by helping the Russians develop the atomic bomb, they were guilty of contributing to the outbreak of the Korean War. He also made clear that while Julius was clearly the main culprit, Ethel was not innocent because of what she knew, and that they had both put their commitment to the Soviet cause above the love for their children. The following day, Morton Sobell was sentenced to thirty years in prison, while David Greenglass was given only fifteen years, undoubtedly because he had helped the prosecution against his sister and brother-in-law.

The judge's claim that the Rosenbergs had given the Russians an atomic advantage is debatable, as is the connection to the Korean War. Whilst Greenglass did give his brother-in-law (and perhaps sister) atomic information, there is no proof that it was truly advantageous to the Russians, and therefore so damaging to the West. Julius Rosenberg's Soviet contact Alexander Feklisov told *The New York Times* in an interview in 1997: 'he didn't understand anything about the atomic bomb and he couldn't help us'. Also, the judge's apportioning of equal blame to Ethel and Julius was based on false testimony, mainly related to Greenglass saying that he saw his sister typing up information for the Russians. As already mentioned, Greenglass said in 2001 that he had not seen his sister typing up such material (of course, this contradicts his original testimony, so it depends on what one believes: Greenglass's original testimony or an interview five decades later). But how innocent could Ethel really have been? Could she have been oblivious to her husband and brother's activities? If she had known, and not been actively involved, that would make her guilty by association, an accessory after the fact. But this charge would surely not have carried the death penalty, even in the era of McCarthyism.

The execution date of the Rosenbergs would be delayed many times. Public protest at the death sentences given to them was fierce and such prominent people as Albert Einstein and Jean-Paul Sartre made clear their opposition to the sentences. Writers, film directors and artists such as Dashiell Hammett (imprisoned by the HUAC earlier for refusing to testify before it), Bertolt Brecht, Fritz Lang, Jean Cocteau, Pablo Picasso, Diego Rivera and Frida Kahlo protested too. Pope Pius XII made an appeal for mercy. Legal arguments would result in many stays of execution. When the official appeal was dismissed, the lawyers appealed directly to President Eisenhower, who refused clemency on 11 February 1953. Julius Rosenberg himself wrote in one of his letters from prison that it was 'a barbaric sentence of death against two innocent people'. The case was on the front page of many newspapers as a new date for the executions was set and then put off again. Julius' mother, Sophie Rosenberg, told the New York *Daily News* on 6 June 1953: 'My son said the papers print lies and he can't get justice! What chance have I got of getting mercy?'

It was not certain that the executions would finally take place until the actual morning of 19 June 1953. On that morning, Julius wrote to his lawyer Emanuel Bloch: 'We are the first victims of American Fascism.' The rest is now history.

Michael and Robert Rosenberg became orphans and were not adopted by any members of their family but by Abel and Anne Meeropol. Abel was a successful songwriter who wrote the anti-racist song *Strange Fruit*, which was sung by Billie Holiday. In his 2008 memoir, Robert Meeropol (the younger of the Rosenbergs' children) said that he and his brother had been happy with their new family. But they never forgot their true parents and spent many years trying to prove their innocence, as did many others. Many books were written about them, portraying them as victims of McCarthyism and anti-Jewish feeling. They became a classic example of American miscarriage of justice.

In 2008, the Grand Jury testimonies from 1950 were released (apart from the testimony of David Greenglass, the release of which was seen as not in the public interest). These were not the testimonies from the main trial itself but from the preliminary hearings used to gather evidence under sworn conditions. There were differences between the Grand Jury testimony of Ruth Greenglass (David's wife) and the testimony she gave at the main trial. The Grand Jury had asked her about the information she and her husband gave to Julius: 'Didn't you write the information down on a piece of paper?' She replied, 'I wrote it down on a piece of paper and Julius took it with him.' At the main trial, she said that Ethel had typed up the information. So why did her testimony change? This may never be known for sure.

Also in 2008, Morton Sobell, by now ninety-one, finally confessed in an interview with *The New York Times* that he had been guilty of espionage and that Julius Rosenberg was part of 'a conspiracy that delivered to the Soviets classified military and industrial information . . . on the atomic bomb'. He stated, however, that the information given by David Greenglass to Julius was 'of little value' to the Russians, and was used to confirm the information acquired by other atomic spies. He also said that Ethel Rosenberg was completely innocent of spying: she had known about her husband Julius' activities but had not actively taken part. If this is true, Ethel should never have been executed.

The case of the Rosenbergs shows how ruthless the world of spying was in the 1950s. But the business of passing secret information is often a matter of life and death, as governments and intelligence agencies strive to protect themselves against enemies. When a spy burrows deep into an intelligence agency, with access to the most crucial information, the damage to that side can be immense, especially if a double agent is at work. The detection of such agents and pre-emptive measures and vetting procedures have grown increasingly sophisticated as lessons have been learnt, often at great cost. George Blake was one double agent whose activities caused significant damage and would become infamous in the annals of espionage.

CHAPTER 6

GEORGE BLAKE

The wall of Wormwood Scrubs Prison in west London was very high. The rope ladder, made of knitting needles, had been thrown over successfully on the third attempt, with perhaps the twentieth rung at the top of the wall. It was 22 October 1966 and England had won the football World Cup just a few months before. The streets had been full of noise then, but they were quieter now. The headlights of passing cars on Artillery Lane occasionally lit up the dusky dimness. A thickset man was standing on a car at the bottom of the ladder, nervously waiting to feel the weight pulling on it. The wall had seemed much higher as he first looked up, but now that the ladder was over it, the top seemed closer somehow. Nothing had prepared him for the adrenaline pumping through him. He climbed off of the car and pulled the ladder away from it further down the wall. Then he heard a scratching sound from the other side. Two sets of fingers appeared at the top. It was starting to spit with rain now. Next a head appeared. The man at the top was wearing only a shirt and he was getting wet, but that was the least of his worries. It was just after 7 p.m.

The man at the bottom of the ladder remonstrated with the man at the top to hurry, and the latter finally heaved himself over, ending up dangling on the outside of the wall upside down. 'Jump!' called the man on the ground. The other man did just that, straightening himself up, but he hit his head on the gravel as he reached the ground. A car's headlights shone in the street. The man standing opened the rear door of the car. Luckily, the man on the ground was obscured by the door, next to the wall. The first man dragged the fallen man into the back seat. 'Are you all right, George?' The man in the back seat only groaned with pain. The headlights of the nearby car had gone out now. Three people got out, but the escape car was already driving away up Du Cane Road.

The man in the back seat was coming to his senses as the rain tapped against the car windows. His name was George Blake. He had just escaped from a forty-two-year prison sentence after serving just under five and a half years for high treason.

George Blake was in fact not British by birth: his mother, Catherine, was Dutch, and his father, Albert Behar, was a Turkish Jew who later became a naturalised British subject. Albert had fought with the British and French against the Ottomans in World War One, with the French decorating him with the prestigious Croix de Guerre and the British with the Military Cross. George Behar was born in Rotterdam, the Netherlands, on 11 November 1922 (he was named George after the British King George V). The Behar family lived reasonably well (Albert was a businessman), but when George was thirteen his father died. George was then sent to live with his aunt in Cairo, Egypt. He attended the English School there, and became close to his cousin, Henri Curiel, who was a communist. It was at this time that George found out that he was half Jewish (people who knew Blake have said he was very shocked that his father had not told him about his origins).

George returned to Holland in the summer of 1939 to visit his mother and sisters. When World War Two broke out in September, his mother decided that he should stay in Holland until things settle down. But on 10 May 1940 the Germans invaded Holland, and soon after the Nazis detained George for a month because he had inherited his father's British citizenship. When released, George discovered that his mother and sisters had been evacuated to Britain. Still a teenager, he went to live with his grandmother and became a messenger for the anti-Nazi Dutch resistance movement. He also delivered under-ground newspapers for them, using the assumed name Max de Vries and false papers. Clearly, he was politicised from a young age, but with the Nazis sweeping through Europe this was perhaps not so uncommon, and of course George was half-Jewish too, a fact that he knew would make him a greater target for the Nazis if his origins were discovered.

In 1942 George's grandmother died. This, and the fact that he was under ever-increasing risk of being interned again (or perhaps eventually sent to a concentration camp) as the Nazi oppression intensified, made up his mind that he had to escape to Britain to join his mother and sisters. But this was easier decided than done. With help from the resistance, he was able to go through Belgium, get to Paris and then Lyon, before moving on to Spain, a journey which took months. However, in Spain he was arrested and once again interned for three months (Spain was then fascist under General Franco). He was finally released in January 1943 because of a combination of the efforts of the British embassy in Madrid and the changing attitude of the Spanish towards the war as a result of the heavy campaign going on in North Africa. With other internees he was taken to Gibraltar and then by ship to Britain.

Reunited with his mother and sisters, George came to live with them in a London suburb and took a desk job with the Dutch government, in exile in London. He was not called up for military service, and after a few months he decided to volunteer himself. It was also at about this time that his family changed their surname by deed poll from Behar to Blake, no doubt to fit more easily into wartime Britain. Indeed, George had undergone a screening process on arrival to judge his allegiance to Britain.

In October 1943, George Blake enlisted in the Royal Navy. He was a month short of his twenty-first birthday. The childhood of George Behar can only be described as turbulent, and it is important not to underestimate the effect that this would have had on his forming personality and outlook on life. George Blake the man was a survivor, who had learnt to be flexible and resourceful, key qualities needed in his later career. But his flexibility and survival instincts also made him fiercely independent and hardened to worldly realities at a young age.

Blake was trained as an officer in the navy, a process that took a year. He was then sent on submarine training to work in two-man submarines, but it was soon discovered that he had a medical problem that made this work dangerous to him (he got oxygen poisoning and fainted). He was withdrawn from submarine work and was recommended by his commanding officer for a post in SIS (now MI6). According to an interview Blake gave to the Russians later (the date of which is unverified), he had several mysterious interviews, and he did not know exactly what he was joining until the final one. This shows that Blake was not trying to penetrate SIS – his recruitment was not manipulated by him, but by circumstances. Unlike Kim Philby, he was not a penetration agent from the beginning.

Since Blake was fluent in Dutch and knew the Netherlands so well, it probably seemed logical to him that he would be sent as an undercover agent to Holland, but SIS had made an agreement with the Dutch that only Dutch subjects would work as agents on Dutch soil. Instead, Blake was sent to 54 Broadway, the headquarters of SIS near St James's Park in London to work in the Dutch section. He helped Dutch agents in training and then moved on to clerical work, translating coded Dutch telegrams. He worked in the office with many members of the British upper class, including female secretaries. In his autobiography, *No Other Choice*, Blake reminisced:

> They were decidedly upper-class and belonged to the higher strata of the establishment. There were among them daughters of Tory MPs and ministers, of bishops, of a Viceroy of India, of court dignitaries and some were even related to the Royal Family.

A former colleague remembered that Blake had a brief love affair with another colleague, Iris Peake. She was the daughter of a Conservative minister, and allegedly her father told Blake after dinner one night that Blake could never marry his daughter (this was because of his background). Much has been made of Blake's hatred of the British class system and snobbery within it, but there is no definitive way of knowing how much this hatred influenced him in his later decision to betray Britain and what it represented.

At the end of the war in May 1945, Blake was offered a permanent post with SIS, and he decided to take it. In an interview with PBS in 1999 he claimed that he briefly went back to Holland to help close down the Dutch agent networks. He was then posted to East Germany (Germany had just been divided) to spy on the Soviet Union, although officially he was still an officer in the Royal Navy. He had to gather any intelligence he could on Soviet activities and help set up a network of agents. After that, he was brought back to London and sent on a Russian language course at Cambridge University. In the PBS interview Blake said that the Russian professor at Cambridge was an English woman whose mother was Russian, and she took him to services of the Russian Orthodox Church and instilled in him a love for Russia. He said that her influence on him was very important as it changed his attitude towards Russia. It didn't affect his views on communism, which were not committed at this time, but it made him sympathetic to Russian people and culture. This was obviously not the trigger that made him a double agent, but it may have had an effect on his later path.

Strangely, having learnt Russian, Blake was then sent to Seoul, South Korea, in October 1948. His task there was to establish another agent network in the coastal regions. He also tried to gain intelligence on North Korea, as it was thought likely that there would be a war, and that the North would win it. The war did break out, but Blake and his colleagues were told to stay in place to observe and gather intelligence. The North Koreans took over Seoul on 24 June 1950, and Blake and the others were interned in small villages. This was when the Americans, British, French and Turkish got involved in the Korean War, under the auspices of the newly founded United Nations.

The North Koreans were communist and had strong links with the Russians. In the PBS interview Blake admitted that he and the other internees met with the Russians regularly while they were held captive. These were outwardly innocuous conversations, where the main subject was the moral rights and wrongs of the Korean War. The Russians also supplied the prisoners with *Das Kapital* to read (Blake admitted that this was an influence on him). The meetings and discussions were obviously a ploy to see if there was anyone who was sufficiently sympathetic to communism (or at least Marxism) to seriously consider working for the Russians.

This tactic was especially clever as the prisoners would have been in a vulnerable state and friendly contact and intellectual stimulation must have been very welcome to them. But Blake said in the interview that he had approached the Russians first, by writing them a note in Russian and sending it to the Soviet embassy in Pen Yang, probably offering his services. According to Blake, he then had several meetings with a KGB colonel (the KGB was formed around this time), while the other prisoners continued their routine meetings with the Russians.

Many writers have felt that Blake was brainwashed while in Korea. But did the Russians really indoctrinate him? This is possible, but Blake himself in the 1999 interview categorically denied that he was brainwashed in any way. He said that it was the devastation meted out by American bombs on North Korean villages and 'defenceless people' that changed his mind about his true allegiance. Of course, as a long-term Soviet agent, Blake would want to say that the decision was his own and one of conscience. He explained that he realised that the way forward was communism, for a fairer, more humane way of life in the future. It was the same argument used by Guy Burgess and Donald Maclean in this period, when opposition to American foreign policy was strong. Whatever the truth, by the time George Blake was released in March 1953 and returned to London after three years in captivity, he was ready to work for the Russians.

Any returning prisoner of war rightly received a hero's welcome; Blake and his fellow prisoners were no exception. There is a photograph of them on arrival, wearing ill-fitting clothes supplied to them. The psychological damage of such internment must have been considerable, but outwardly Blake showed little change in his personality, apart from the usual period of readjustment required. It is important to remember that Blake had previously suffered capture and internment by the Germans and the Spanish, although for much shorter periods.

Blake began to have meetings with his new KGB contact Nikolai Korovin. They met in The Hague, Holland, and perhaps even at Otpor, between Peking and Moscow. In September 1953, Blake went back to active service with SIS. He had been made the deputy head of the prestigious Section Y, which dealt with information obtained by the tapping of telephones in Vienna. One early evening in October, he met Korovin outside Belsize Park underground station in north London. Blake wrote in his autobiography that Korovin tended to leave his home early in the morning and spend all day making criss-crossing journeys across London to shake his tails before an evening rendezvous, as he was known to MI5 (he was under diplomatic cover). This was a similar tactic used by Kim Philby in the early 1950s, and was obviously a classic KGB technique. Blake said that this system never failed to work. It is probable that Blake handed over all of the information that passed his desk while in Section Y.

By this time Blake had an English wife and

children, but family life would not change him. His career in SIS and his double-agent activities would come first, although in the PBS interview he admitted he felt guilty that his espionage and work for SIS affected his first marriage and his relationship with his children.

In January 1955, Blake was once again on the move, alone (his family stayed in England), when he was posted to Berlin, a very sensitive intelligence station in those early days of the Cold War, as it was divided between East and West. He had a new Soviet contact and met with him on a regular basis. Ironically, Blake's main task for the SIS was to recruit Soviet and East German double agents. It was in Germany, during his four-and-a-half-year stay, that Blake did his greatest damage as a double agent. One of the biggest secrets that Blake supplied to the Russians were the details of the Allied technical project known as GOLD.

GOLD was basically a complex eavesdropping system developed by the Allies under the streets of Berlin to listen to the Russians' operational plans within their controlled segment of the city. The idea had previously been developed under the streets of Vienna (much of this information had been interpreted by Blake in Section Y in London and passed to the Russians). The Vienna project had been code-named SILVER. It had been so productive (though sometimes probably counter-productive, with Blake informing the Russians) that it had been decided to develop a similar underground network in Berlin too. GOLD was a joint project with the CIA, and meant digging a tunnel under Berlin's streets almost half a mile (0.8 km) long. By tapping into the Soviet telephone and telegraph cables underground, the British and Americans were able to intercept and record every telephone call and telegram into and out of the Soviet zone of Berlin. This gave the Allies the enormous strategic advantage of knowing the next moves to be taken by the Russians, both political and military. Or at least it would have been a huge advantage if Blake hadn't given the Russians all the details of the project.

The preparation of GOLD was very expensive, and because the scheme was technically complicated, it had taken years of research. It was often claimed that the tunnel had not yet been started when Blake informed the Russians. But the Mitrokhin Archive shows that the West had already taken 50,000 reels of tape with recorded information before the project was abandoned when the Russians pretended to accidentally find out about GOLD in April 1956. Blake himself confirmed in the PBS interview that the tunnel had operated for eleven months. SIS and the CIA put the Russians' discovery down to a technical fault caused by heavy rain, so Blake's espionage was not exposed, but one of the messages recorded by GOLD told of a Soviet agent working for the British in Berlin. It would take almost another five years before the agent was confirmed as Blake, and by then he had done further damage.

It was a very sensitive political time, just before the signing of the Warsaw Pact, and it is not an overstatement to say that Blake's information about GOLD changed the course of the Cold War. Blake had removed the West's advantage and may have given the Allies a disadvantage if the Russians ran false information through the system (this has never been definitively confirmed). This one act of espionage alone made Blake one of the most damaging spies of the century.

But there was more. During his time in Berlin, Blake told the Russians about at least one, if not two, of their own operatives who were helping the West. Piotr Popov was working for the CIA, and Blake's information led to his capture by the Russians. Blake may well have also given the Russians information that later led to the arrest of Oleg Penkovsky (see Chapter Eight). Claims have also been made by the secret services that Blake betrayed the identities of up to four hundred SIS agents. If this is true, then he undoubtedly sent British agents to their deaths. So while Ian Fleming was busy writing the early James Bond novels, Blake was possibly sealing the fates of secret agents. He may not have used a gun, a knife or his hands like Bond, but he might have been fatally compromising those agents with his information. The fact that Blake was also tall, dark and handsome meant that there would be inevitable comparisons with James Bond later, even if he was working for two sides at once – or, as he would say, only Russia.

In the summer of 1959 Blake was transferred back to London. He worked in the Victoria area, not far from SIS headquarters at 54 Broadway. His job was to evaluate and recruit potential secret agents amongst British businessmen travelling abroad, as their business gave them a perfect cover. Blake was back in contact with Nikolai Korovin (and sometimes Korovin's assistant) in London, continuing to pass along any information he learned. He remained until September 1960, when he was posted to Lebanon, where he was to learn Arabic for a future assignment, at the Middle East Centre for Arabic Studies (MECAS) near Beirut. He was there for six months when he was suddenly recalled back to London.

Unknown to Blake, events had been conspiring against him in his absence. Firstly, there was evidence that he had been close to Horst Eitner, a German agent that he had controlled in West Berlin for SIS who had since been arrested for being a Soviet agent. Blake was considered contaminated by his close association. But the second piece of evidence against him was far more damaging. A Polish agent working for the Russians called Michal Goleniewski had defected, and he informed SIS that there had been a double agent working for SIS in Berlin. Documents had been leaked over years, and after an investigation Blake was found to have been the source of one of the documents. Given also the collapse of GOLD, SIS were now focused on Blake, but their evidence was largely circumstantial. To prosecute, SIS would need a confession.

Blake had no idea why he had suddenly been called back to London. There were rumours of a possible promotion, and he certainly had no suspicion that he was under scrutiny. Once in London, he was told of the suspicions against him and then underwent intensive interrogation for days. But Blake did not break easily. He was now a seasoned pro, and he was cunning and resilient. Blake claimed in his autobiography that he broke down only when he was accused of taking money from the Russians, a low blow to his ideological pride. But the truth seems to be that he made an elementary mistake whilst under mounting pressure. During breaks in his interrogation, he was allowed to wander off in London for his lunch. On the first day he was not followed; it is likely that SIS were trying to lull him into a false sense of security. On the second day, he was kept under surveillance, and he did exactly what they hoped he would do: he cracked under pressure. He was seen approaching a public telephone box, circling it, and then changing his mind. It was obvious that he was considering calling his Soviet contact Nikolai Korovin in a panic. He may have thought better of it, but this gave SIS more leverage when the interrogation resumed. Was he going to call his contact to arrange his rescue? Blake finally cracked. He was taken to a small house in the country, where he was held under guard for the weekend, until SIS decided how to proceed with him. He was formally arrested on 10 April 1961.

The trial of George Blake began on 3 May and only took a day. Blake pleaded guilty and expected to receive a sentence of fourteen years for his spying, as Britain had not been technically at war after Korea (although some would argue that the Cold War was a war of a kind). However, Lord Chief Justice Parker sentenced him to forty-two years' imprisonment, fourteen years for each charge of spying against him, to run consecutively.

This was the longest prison sentence ever handed out by a British court with regard to the actual sentence conferred, although it was later supplanted by the forty-five year sentence given to a terrorist for the attempted bombing of an aeroplane. Blake's sentence made all the front pages of the newspapers. The length of it was shocking to many. Apparently, Blake collapsed in court when he heard it, but he later said that he was pleased that the sentence was so long, as the length was so unreal that he could not think about it realistically, which allowed him to live with it more easily.

SIS and MI5 continued to interview Blake in Wormwood Scrubs Prison, where he was kept in the high-security wing. It was important for the British to know exactly what he had given to the Russians (almost everything he was able to) and also to learn anything they could about the Soviet espionage structure in Britain. Blake identified his Soviet contacts during these 'debriefing' sessions that would last more than a year. Meanwhile the newspapers were having a field day. For example, the *Daily Express* of 20 June 1961, when Blake lost his appeal, claimed that Blake had received one year for every British agent he had betrayed to the Russians. In prison, Blake adapted well to his sentence. His ability to live in solitude was a great advantage to him; his three years as a prisoner in Korea and shorter interments had already conditioned his personality to survive in similar conditions. However, such a long prison sentence must have been extremely daunting.

The resilience of his character, forged by a turbulent life, and his professional training as a spy had no doubt hardened him. In Wormwood Scrubs he sewed mailbags in the mailbag shop and to occupy his mind he studied Arabic literature. There was also a deep spiritual and solitary side to Blake, and he read many religious and philosophical texts. He was known as a good listener, helping others with problems and giving advice. Another prisoner said that Blake showed no indications of panic, no obvious outward sign of being crushed by the weight of his sentence. But Blake had learnt to internalise his emotions over the years.

During exercise periods, Blake was also able to

meet Gordon Lonsdale (real name Konon Molody) and Peter Kroger (real name Morris Cohen), other Russian spies recently arrested by MI5 as part of the Portland Spy Ring. Molody was serving twenty-five years and Cohen twenty years. The Portland spies had been tried in March 1961 before the same judge that sentenced Blake two months later, but they pleaded not guilty. The fact that Blake was able to speak to both of these men (only briefly and by accident) would be controversial later – spies should not have been able to fraternise together.

While Blake was undoubtedly a model prisoner and popular with other inmates (perhaps surprising due to what he had done in their eyes), it should not be underestimated how manipulative he could be. He was a naturally crafty character who was skilful at getting others on his side, and it was obviously in his interests to do that in prision. In September 1965, having served just over four years of his sentence, Blake made his move. He had struck up a casual friendship with another prisoner, a thirty-two-year-old Irishman called Sean Bourke, who was coming to the end of his sentence. Bourke had served seven years for allegedly sending a letter bomb to a British policeman; he had pleaded not guilty and always said that he was innocent of the crime. He was a colourful character, fond of drinking, and in prison he had slowly graduated to the privileged job of editing the prisoners' magazine. He was not housed in the high-security hall D, as Blake was, but his editorial office was there, so Blake had a chance to get to know him a little.

Bourke had had a troubled youth and was very anti-authority. Blake obviously picked up on this, and he knew that Bourke would soon be released. Having known Bourke for some time and with nothing to lose, he approached him for his help in escaping. Blake had judged Bourke well – the Irishman promised to help in this very risky operation. Blake had obviously given up hope of the Russians getting him over the wall, and he must have realised that he had to arrange something himself if he wasn't to stay in prison until old age. When Bourke was released (first to a readjustment hostel and then completely), he set about his difficult task. He met with Blake's mother to ask her to help finance the escape. She refused, so he had to find other backers. This is where the details become murky.

Bourke had served some of his time in prison with Michael Randle and Pat Pottle, two men who had been arrested for their protest activities as members of the Committee of 100, the anti-nuclear protest group set up by the philosopher Bertrand Russell. They had been arrested for public disorder for a demonstration at an RAF base and in December 1962 they were sentenced to eighteen months. After serving their sentence, they had been released. Bourke approached them both and asked for their help. After thinking about it, they agreed. They both had left-wing sympathies and felt that Blake's forty-two-year sentence was unjust (they would lay out their motives in their joint memoir *The Blake Escape*, published in 1989, when they were named publicly; they would stand trial but never be convicted for their part in Blake's escape).

According to the espionage writer Nigel West, the money needed for the operation was raised through other contacts in the Committee of 100. There were some famous names in the group, and West claims that the famous film director Tony Richardson (who directed *A Taste of Honey* and many other films) was instrumental. Allegedly, Richardson had been persuaded to finance the escape by the Reverend John Papworth, who at the time was the vicar of a church in North London and had previously stood as a parliamentary candidate for the Labour Party. It is estimated that the cost was seven or eight hundred pounds, a considerable sum in 1965–66. When the escape was being planned, Richardson had recently divorced the well-respected actress Vanessa Redgrave, also famous for her left-wing sympathies, who would be questioned by MI5 in the late 1960s. This author attempted to contact Vanessa Redgrave through her agent in late 2008, to ask if she had any knowledge of her ex-husband's alleged financial help in the escape, but received no reply. During a phone conversation, Reverend John Papworth denied ever meeting Tony Richardson.

However, once the money was procured, Sean Bourke could begin to plan the escape. He bought a two-way radio set, and one of the radios was smuggled into Blake in Wormwood Scrubs. Using a calling code, Blake and Bourke were able to communicate regularly at night to plan the escape, which is quite incredible considering that Blake was supposed to be in a high-security confinement. They planned to execute the escape on the night of the prison film club, and Blake began to attend the club. Bourke was very professional in his planning, with the help of Randle and Pottle, and the only amateur touch was the ladder he made. Blake finally went over the wall on 22 October 1966.

The reaction in the newspapers was intense and the manhunt was on. All the ports and airports were put under surveillance, but in reality Blake was hidden by Bourke in a small lodging room just a few streets away from Wormwood Scrubs. Blake had hurt his wrist in the fall from the wall, and it was treated secretly by a sympathetic doctor. Blake would remain at various London addresses for two months, before he was spirited out of Britain in a specially adapted van, hiding in a secret compartment. Michael Randle drove the van to the continent with his family, and in East Berlin Blake was welcomed by the KGB, who were amazed at his escape with the help of amateurs.

Sean Bourke would go to Berlin himself in January 1967, as the heat was firmly on him by now. He would join Blake in Moscow and stay there for almost a year, writing his memoir, *The Springing of George Blake*. In Moscow, Bourke fell out with Blake, and he claimed in his book that he overheard a conversation between Blake and a KGB officer in which it was being decided whether Bourke should be forced to stay in Moscow or perhaps be liquidated. Bourke managed to get back to Ireland, and MI5 were unsuccessful in their attempts to extradite him from Dublin. In the meantime, the KGB had seized his manuscript and he later received through the post a version which had been heavily edited when it came to his time in Moscow. The book was published in Britain in 1970 and made Bourke a lot of money, which he largely drank away. He was never prosecuted for helping Blake escape, and he died in 1982.

Blake has lived in Moscow on a KGB pension since his escape, and it seems that he adapted well to his new life. He got married to a Russian woman and they became good friends with Kim Philby and his wife. There is a famous photograph of the four of them together at a dacha outside Moscow some time in the 1970s. Blake's three sons regularly went to see him in Moscow from the early 1980s, and he published his autobiography, originally called *No Abiding City* but renamed *No Other Choice* when published in Britain in 1990 (MI5 seized the royalties from this book).

On his eighty-fifth birthday in November 2007, George Blake was given the prestigious decoration the Order of Friendship by then president Vladimir Putin.

George Blake had certainly experienced great turmoil and instability in his early life, which helped to mould his character into that of a hardened, resilient survivor. The early death of his father and the move to Cairo, the influence of his cousin Henri Curiel (later a prominent member of the Communist Party of Egypt and suspiciously murdered in 1978) and the periods of internment as a youth all undoubtedly had a strong impact on his personality and future direction. However, it was his time as a prisoner in Korea that was the turning point – perhaps with the added cajoling of the Soviets. Cunning and manipulative, Black was perhaps a perfect spy. But there can be no doubt that – like Kim Philby, Donald Maclean and Klaus Fuchs – Blake had an ideology which enabled him to make the sacrifices and take the risks he did.

In *No Other Choice*, Blake sheds light on the development of his ideology. Although the Soviet Union had recently collapsed when he wrote the autobiography, he still believed in the core ideas of communism, despite acknowledging that the 'experiment' had failed in practice. He writes that although the communist experiment in Russia had not worked in the long term, it was because it was applied by 'force' and 'terror' and that the system would only work if applied peacefully as a 'natural process of spiritual growth'. Blake then poses the question of whether the entire experiment, and the untold suffering that resulted, was all in vain, and he answers it by saying that every change in history – whether that of empires, the French Revolution, the industrial revolution or world religions – has required great suffering and sacrifice. There is no doubt that Blake is unrepentant about his espionage and still firmly believes that what he did was for a good cause – for the best for humanity in general. He has kept this faith despite the great corruption and inequalities and despite the collapse of the Soviet Union. Blake is the classic crusader. He embarked on his path in Korea and never looked back.

The world of espionage is a murky place, where underhand methods and manipulations are used as a matter of course. Often the end justifies the means. Such Machiavellian methods have been used by every intelligence service representing a government at one time or another. Gaining access to government secrets by recruiting a spy is often about identifying an individual's weakness in society, exploiting it and using it to gain a foothold within the enemy camp – as John Vassall was to learn.

CHAPTER 7

JOHN VASSALL

On the evening of 19 March 1955, there was a formal ball being held at the American Club in Moscow, largely for the American and British diplomatic community. But John Vassall, a thirty-year-old assistant naval attaché, had decided not to go. It was a decision he would regret for the rest of his life.

Vassall was a junior diplomat who had begun to fit into the vastly different Russian culture since arriving at the British embassy in Moscow in March 1954, almost exactly a year earlier. At first Vassall had been something of an outsider at the embassy. In a report written soon after his arrival, his boss, Captain Bennett, mentioned 'his handicap of an irritating, effeminate personality'. But Vassall had since managed to build a good relationship with Bennett and his wife.

That night, instead of attending the ball at the American Club, Vassall was going to spend time with a friend of a friend, a Russian soldier apparently home on leave. After meeting the soldier in a Moscow street as arranged, Vassall and his new friend went back to the soldier's flat, where they were soon making love. In his autobiography, *Vassall*, published in 1975, he looked back on that fateful night: 'I found a kind of sanctuary in his arms, as he held me, saying hardly a word. There was nothing faked about his lovemaking.' What Vassall did not know was that it was a KGB trap. He and the soldier were being photographed, and after a while the door from the next room opened.

Two KGB officers entered while the soldier quickly got dressed and left the room without saying anything. Vassall was then allowed to dress and was taken into the next room. The KGB officers showed him graphic photographs of his lovemaking, including oral and anal sex in the course of that night. Of course, homosexuality was then illegal and scandalous in both Russia and Britain. Vassall knew that he couldn't claim diplomatic immunity for this reason. The KGB officers interrogated him, one asking if he were a spy for SIS, which he truthfully denied. Vassall later wrote how one of the officers threatened him by stating plain facts: 'I was told that I had committed a grave offence under Soviet law and that I was in serious trouble with the State.' This was somewhat ironic as the Cambridge spy Guy Burgess was then living in Moscow, enjoying various homosexual affairs to which the recently formed KGB turned a blind eye.

In another version of the events, which Vassall told to Special Branch interrogators in 1962, the incriminating evidence came from an orgy involving two or three Russians, also in a private flat after a dinner near the Bolshoi Ballet. Vassall said in his statement that over dinner he was given brandy, and then everybody took off their jackets. Someone helped him remove his own. Soon they were all naked, and two or three of them got on a bed in the corner of the room where 'certain compromising sexual actions' occurred, and he was aware of somebody taking photographs.

Whatever the exact truth, Vassall was finally allowed to return home in the middle of the night and warned not to tell anyone. The following evening he was picked up a few streets away from his home by a KGB limousine and the process continued. Within days, Vassall was passing top-secret documents from the British embassy to the KGB so that they could be photographed before being returned.

It was a classic case of entrapment by blackmail.

John Vassall's father, William, came from a long line of clergy. He was the chaplain to St Bartholomew's Hospital in London, where he met and married a nurse who would give birth to their first child, William John Christopher Vassall, on 20 September 1924. Another son would follow a year and a half later, giving John (as he preferred to be called, instead of William) a younger brother. In 1925, John's father became vicar to Christ Church in Hendon, North London, where the family would remain for fifteen years. In 1940, his mother had a crisis of religious confidence and converted to Roman Catholicism (John would do the same in 1953, a year before being posted to Moscow). This sudden religious conversion changed the way the family lived. Reverend Vassall was forced to resign his vicarage when his flock protested at his wife's change of heart. He became a chaplain in the RAF. Meanwhile, John, a bright boy, had been attending Monmouth Grammar School, but as his father's income significantly decreased, he had to leave at the age of sixteen. He had to go straight into work.

John Vassall worked in a bank and as a temporary junior clerk at the Admiralty for a short time before joining the RAF and training as a photographer, a pursuit for which he showed aptitude. When he left the RAF after the war, in 1947, he got a job with the Admiralty again as a clerical officer. He went on to work in the Air Equipment Department, Naval Law Department and then the War Registry. It was while working at the registry that he applied for the post of assistant naval attaché at the British embassy in Moscow.

John was artistic, delicate and slightly effeminate. He was also homosexual, but he did not share this with his family and friends, as such inclinations had to be well guarded in 1940s Britain. He liked to spend time with elderly ladies, and he was kind and attentive to them (one of them would allude to his homosexuality in a reference she provided for the Admiralty, writing that he showed no interest in the opposite sex). He was sociable, enjoyed playing bridge, but even at this early stage he was compartmentalising his life. He was also becoming increasingly religious, attending church every Sunday and becoming a Roman Catholic, but incredibly never telling his mother about this. Rebecca West, in her book *The Meaning of Treason*, wrote that Vassall was active on the gay scene before he went to Moscow, secretly enjoying affairs with many partners. This flirtatiousness, which West described as his 'girlish' manner, was something that the KGB no doubt picked up on later.

Why did Vassall apply to go to Moscow? There is no definite answer, but it could well have been just for adventure, to travel and see the world; Russia at that time was far more alien to Westerners than it is today. There is no evidence whatsoever that Vassall ever showed any communist leaning or sympathies. In his autobiography, he did not explain his motives. Could he have become an agent in London before going to Moscow and then tried to penetrate the British embassy there? There is no evidence of this, and it is extremely unlikely. For one thing, the KGB would probably have ordered him to continue with his job at the War Registry (the Admiralty's communications department at that time) and spy for them there. It is also unlikely that Vassall would have sought out espionage on his own. He was something of a nervous, neurotic man, and without any ideological motive there seems little chance that he would have made the first move.

Following interviews and the taking up of his references (the insinuation about his homosexuality by the elderly referee was not followed up by the Admiralty), Vassall was on his way to Moscow. After acclimatising to the very different way of life and settling into the very stiff atmosphere there, he made friends, including with a young Russian interpreter. According to the writer Roger Wilkes, the British ambassador to Moscow later remembered Vassall patronisingly as being 'an obliging little figure who was useful at tea parties', and this description fits in with his patient and ingratiating manner when befriending elderly ladies.

After his entrapment in March 1955, Vassall continued to pass documents to the Russians in Moscow. He was working in the Naval Intelligence Division, so he had access to a great deal of secret material. He was recalled to London in July 1956, having served his term. But his usefulness to the Russians was far from over.

Vassall had not returned directly to London. On the way he stopped in the United States, Canada, Norway and Sweden. This had nothing to do with his espionage; he was just satisfying his wanderlust – a young man seeing the world. What it highlights is the financial arrangement that must have taken place. Vassall was a junior member of staff, and back at the Admiralty in London his salary was about fifteen pounds a week. It's clear that the KGB were paying him: apparently fifty pounds on at least one occasion in Moscow and fees running into hundreds of pounds back in London over the following six years, according to his obituary in *The Daily Telegraph*.

In London, Vassall moved back in with his parents. He would remain there, travelling to work at the Admiralty every morning, until April 1959, when he moved into a block of flats called Hood House in Dolphin Square, Pimlico, an exclusive area next to the Thames and close to Buckingham Palace. Other occupants of these flats over the years have included Charles de Gaulle, Sir Oswald Mosley, Harold Wilson and Christine Keeler (see Chapter Nine). Vassall's flat offered had a view of the central garden and consisted of a lounge and a small bedroom and kitchen. In his autobiography, Vassall wrote: 'It was a great pleasure at last to have a place of my own, where I could entertain my friends from abroad and return some of the generous hospitality I had received.'

The rent was three hundred and fifty pounds a year plus rates, around four hundred pounds in total. This was a sizeable amount, considering that his annual salary was less than eight hundred pounds a year. There would later be some queries raised as to whether Vassall's employment reference to the landlord had been followed up, as surely the Admiralty or the landlord would have questioned how he could have afforded to rent such a flat. Vassall led his colleagues to believe that he had inherited private money from a relative, and they saw no reason to question this at the time. He lived a seemingly privileged life, throwing many parties at his small but exquisitely decorated and furnished flat. Behind his back, his colleagues called him 'Aunty Vera of the Admiralty', in reference to his camp manner. Vassall was a man who liked to live well, and for the first time in his life he could afford to do so, with the Russians perhaps almost doubling his salary secretly.

It is probable that while in Moscow and at first back in London, Vassall was passing crucial NATO secrets to the KGB. This would be largely to do with NATO naval exercises that the Russians would have been keen to learn about. In London the KGB supplied Vassall with a camera, and he began to photograph the documents himself (his professional photography training in the RAF would have undoubtedly come in useful here). He would take documents at random (he wasn't asked to be selective), smuggle them out of the Admiralty in a briefcase (sometimes even in a magazine) and photograph them that night in Dolphin Square, before returning them the next day to their rightful place. It is estimated that he took around a hundred and forty documents out in this way in those London years, many of them dealing with weapons development, specifically new torpedo designs, radar innovations and anti-submarine equipment and armaments.

Vassall had to meet his KGB contact, 'Gregory', regularly to pass over the photographed material.

They met in various designated places, the main ones being a Greek Restaurant on the Cockfosters Road and Frognal Station on north London's Finchley Road. There was also a prearranged place near Holland Park, where Vassall could leave a signal if he wanted to meet his contact urgently (this simple procedure was still being used by the KGB and CIA in operations thirty years later in other countries). In his confession, released to the public in 2006, Vassall explained the procedure: 'Gregory arranged with me that if I wanted to contact him urgently I would leave a circle in pink chalk on a wooden fence directly above the trunk of a tree . . . I only made use of this on one or two occasions.' There was also another way to make quick contact, straight out of a spy novel: Vassall had to call the telephone number Kensington 8955 and ask to speak to 'Miss Mary'. He said that he had cause to call 'Miss Mary' only once.

Vassall soon earned a promotion, and he was made personal secretary to the Civil Lord of the Admiralty, the Scottish MP Thomas (Tam) Galbraith. In 1959, Galbraith moved to the Scottish Office department, which was based in London, and Vassall transferred with him. This would give Vassall even easier access to photographing secret documents, as part of his job was to transport such documents to Galbraith at his homes in both Scotland and London – which meant that he was now taking them out of the office overtly. Questions about an alleged close relationship between Vassall and Galbraith would arise later.

But Vassall's luck was beginning to run out. In January 1961, MI5 arrested the members of the Portland Spy Ring and found a microfilm of documents that came from the Admiralty. This did not point to Vassall directly. However, as a consequence, the KGB told him to stop operating for a while, and he didn't resume his spying again until 1962, photographing his last document in September of that year. Events out of both his and the KGB's control were moving fast. There were two Soviet defectors at this time: Anatoli Golitsyn and Yuri Nosenko. Golitsyn went to the CIA first and began to be debriefed, conclusively fingering Kim Philby and throwing up evidence of an Admiralty spy. The latter information was also confirmed by Vassall's former workplace, the British embassy in Moscow, which verified that Vassall had had access to such documents, as the Russians were found to have material that could only have come from the Admiralty in London. Yuri Nosenko approached the CIA in June 1962 and to prove his worth gave them some information that strengthened the evidence for the existence of an Admiralty spy. Although Nosenko did not actually defect until January 1964 (unfortunately for him, he was then imprisoned for some time by the CIA as Golitsyn had warned the Americans that the KGB might send some defector 'plants', as the Mitrokhin Archive states). The CIA contacted MI5, and the hunt for the Admiralty mole was on.

It was not long before Vassall was in MI5's sights. But it was Special Branch, not MI5, that got him. On 12 September 1962, just days after passing his last document, Vassall was arrested and asked to hand over the keys to his flat in Dolphin Square. Apparently he did this without the slightest hesitation. Amid expensive furniture, designer suits hanging in the wardrobe, exclusive perfumes and pictures of rugged French rugby players, the Special Branch found what they were looking for. Inside an antique piece of furniture, there was a secret compartment, and inside it was the KGB camera and copies of photographs Vassall had taken. There was little point in denying anything, and Vassall quickly confessed.

When Prime Minister Harold Macmillan was informed, he was livid, exclaiming, 'Oh that's bad news, very bad news.' He was especially aware that the homosexual element would produce a media feeding frenzy. He was right: the newspapers had a field day with the story, and just before his trial Vassall was amazingly able to sell his personal account to the *Sunday Pictorial* newspaper for five thousand pounds, an enormous sum then. It appeared under the headline 'Why I betrayed my country' and was accompanied by photographs of Vassall not wearing a shirt. This added to the furore. The spate of spy scandals – the Portland

Spy Ring and George Blake made the news not long before – had risen to a simmering point, and Vassall's exposure, magnified greatly by the then scandalous nature of homosexuality, was prime fuel for the tabloids. In her book *The Meaning of Treason*, reissued just a few years after the Vassall affair, Rebecca West deconstructs some of the inaccurate stories served up by the newspapers in 1962.

One insinuated that Vassall had enjoyed more than just a professional relationship with his boss, Minister Thomas Galbraith. Some photographs of Galbraith were found in Vassall's flat; they were not intimate, but showed a social relationship. The report alluded to more, along with rumours that Galbraith had visited Vassall's flat. Galbraith was forced to defend himself, and on 23 October, six weeks after Vassall's arrest, he told the *Daily Mail* that his relationship with John Vassall was 'no different from those with other civil servants'. To answer the question of why he had not questioned Vassall's apparently high standard of living in contrast to his modest salary, Galbraith repeated the reason given by many of Vassall's colleagues: he thought that Vassall had inherited some money. In response to media rumours, Galbraith went even further on 1 November, issuing a statement through his solicitors that he had never known about Vassall's homosexuality. But that was not to be the end of it. The leaders of the opposition Labour Party, Hugh Gaitskell and George Brown, decided to probe further, knowing that this would damage Macmillan's Conservative government, already smarting from spy exposures. They began raising the issue in Parliament, demanding answers. The questions were fielded by the minister of defence, Peter Thorneycroft, who somewhat unwisely treated them in a rather patrician manner; when asked how Vassall had been able to live like he did, Thorneycroft replied: 'How many of us are living above our incomes in London squares?'

However, it was the link to Thomas Galbraith that kept the newspapers busy. The government set up an internal inquiry into the Vassall affair, and the *Sunday Pictorial* were sent some letters and postcards written by Vassall and Galbraith to each other when they were employee and employer. It is unknown how the paper came to possess them, but Vassall himself could have been responsible. The correspondence was actually very innocent, dealing with work matters, but one particular postcard to Vassall from Galbraith when he was on holiday in Italy fed the rumours. It was all the *Daily Mail* needed to write that the postcard displayed 'a friendliness which one would not expect to exist between a clerk and a senior colleague'. Today this appears a relatively innocent statement, but at the time it was knowingly heavy with insinuation. Within days, Galbraith resigned, stating in his letter of resignation that he felt that he was becoming an embarrassment to the government due to the media interest. He would re-emerge as the parliamentary under-secretary at the Department of Transport in May 1963, before falling with the Macmillan government in the following year. Galbraith never held high office again but remained a Member of Parliament until his death in 1982. He was not the only political casualty of the Vassall affair though. In 1996, the MP Sir Fergus Montgomery revealed that he had been forced to resign as Margaret Thatcher's private parliamentary secretary in 1976 because other colleagues had discovered that he had been a friend of Vassall in 1961, a full fifteen years earlier.

Back in November 1962, Galbraith's boss, the First Lord of the Admiralty Lord Carrington, was next to come under fire. The *Daily Express* alleged that Carrington had known that there had been a spy in his department but had done nothing about it for a year and a half. This could have been truly damaging to the government, even if not true, as rumours sometimes stay in the minds of the public. Macmillan acted fast, setting up a fully independent inquiry under Lord Radcliffe into the Vassall affair, making the matter *sub judice* and barring the newspapers from reporting on it.

The results of the inquiry were published on 25 April 1963 as the *Report of the Tribunal Appointed to Inquire into the Vassall Case and Related Matters*. Both Lord Carrington and Thomas Galbraith. Regarding Thomas Galbraith: 'There was nothing improper in the relationship between Mr Galbraith and Vassall.' Galbraith received damages for defamation from a newspaper group. Regarding Lord Carrington: 'There is no truth in the allegation that the presence of another spy inside the Admiralty was known to the first lord and his Service chiefs for eighteen months before Vassall's arrest. The first suspicion of this was conveyed to them in April 1962.' Largely in response to Harold Macmillan's criticisms of the media's handling of the Vassall affair, two journalists were imprisoned for six months and three months respectively for refusing to divulge their sources about Vassall to the inquiry. But this would come back to haunt Macmillan: the following year the Profumo Affair would give the newspapers a chance for revenge (see Chapter Nine).

Vassall himself was in prison. His trial at the Old Bailey was held mainly in secret. Vassall was sentenced to eighteen years, but he was a model prisoner and served only ten years, being released in 1972. He went on to publish his frank autobiography in 1975 and later changed his name to John Phillips. He became a clerk at the British Records Association and lived out the rest of his life in anonymity. He died of a heart attack outside an underground station in London on 18 November 1996. He was seventy-one years old, and nobody had heard from him for years. But the round of obituaries proved how significant his earlier life had been.

★   ★   ★

'The selection of Vassall, a weak, vain individual and a practising homosexual, for appointment as Naval Attache's clerk in Moscow can now be seen to be the decisive mistake in the history of this case.' So reads the 1963 tribunal inquiry report into the Vassall case. It is a document of its time, especially in its attitudes towards homosexuality. But it also shows itself to be less than penetrating about the failings of the Admiralty to vet its staff at the crucial early days of the Cold War. For instance, it tells us that the 'security re-vetting' of Vassall before being posted to Moscow in 1954 was just a check of his name on MI5 and SIS records. He was being posted to perhaps the most sensitive embassy in the world (along with Berlin), and that was the extent of his vetting. As the report reveals elsewhere, Vassall was not subject to 'Positive Vetting', a far more rigorous process. In 1954, this type applied only to 'those officials with access to atomic secrets or strategic and technical plans'. But the report later informs us that Vassall had had access to these very secrets in his career.

The report states: 'Vassall had little authorised access, certainly in recent years, to information about NATO sea exercises.' This access surely included 'strategic plans', which were stipulated to require positive vetting, and the term 'certainly in recent years' is hardly reassuring. 'Vassall's later role in the Naval Intelligence Division was as "Atomic Liaison Officer" – one of his duties – but he had limited access to secrets for any length of time.' But how much time did Vassall need to pass the documents to the KGB to be photographed, or later, back in London, to photograph them himself? The report also confirms that after January 1962, when he was in the Military Branch, Vassall had increased access to documents: 'Vassall was for short periods the personal assistant to the head of his section. This gave him access to more valuable documents than he was usually privy to.' So after a brief hiatus from spying under KGB orders after the exposure of the Portland Spy Ring and George Blake, he was able to pass on sensitive information to the Russians.

The report places the blame firmly on Vassall's shoulders and exonerates his superiors and the Admiralty completely. Lord Carrington may not have known that there was a spy in the Admiralty for eighteen months, as the newspapers reported in November 1962, and Vassall's direct boss, Thomas Galbraith, may not have had an inappropriate relationship with him. But the Admiralty and the government were obviously guilty as institutions – the former for failing to vet staff thoroughly and the latter for closing ranks when blame was being apportioned.

With regard to Vassall's homosexuality, the tribunal report states: 'Although many of Vassall's colleagues in the Admiralty regarded him as effeminate, there was little suspicion by any of them that he might be a homosexual.' This is difficult to believe. The KGB had no problem identifying him as homosexual and entrapping him using this knowledge, and it's worth remembering that apparently some of Vassall's colleagues nicknamed him 'Aunty Vera of the Admiralty'. Brendan Mulholland of the *Daily Mail* reported this in 1962, and he was later to serve six months in prison for refusing to divulge his source for this information to the tribunal. As already mentioned, there is also the fact that one of Vassall's referees for the Moscow job, an elderly lady acquaintance, had subtly implied that Vassall showed 'little interest in the opposite sex'. It is highly possible that the Admiralty were not unduly worried about Vassall's homosexuality if they knew. When Vassall joined the Admiralty, it may not have been apparent that such potential weakness could lead to ruthless blackmailing on the part of the Russians: his was the first high-profile KGB homosexual blackmailing case.

Regardless of the lax vetting procedures or any fault that may be assigned to the Admiralty, the fact is that the KGB had trapped John Vassall in a very professional way. The KGB had been formed in the month that Vassall arrived at the British embassy in Moscow, and the tactics they used on him a year later, in March 1955, were new and more brutal than the tactics employed in penetrating enemy intelligence services until that time. All the evidence points to the fact that Vassall had no ideological leaning towards communism and his recruitment occurred against his will. But not everybody has taken this view. The writer Rebecca West has claimed that Vassall might well have been guiltier than he appeared. In *The Meaning of Treason*, she puts forward the idea that he approached the Russians before applying for the Moscow post, and that this could have been a case of the Soviets grooming him to move into position (very much like they had with the Cambridge spies twenty years earlier). This is possible, but there is no hard evidence.

The behaviour of Vassall after he was entrapped speaks for itself. He appeared to revel in his lifestyle and showed little sign of strain to his colleagues. Being blackmailed would surely have produced a great feeling of bitterness. This anger probably would have subsided over time, but would a man who had been forced into a very dangerous game have been able to operate so well, taking documents out in magazines? Of course, Vassall had a lot to lose. Being exposed as a homosexual (with the incontrovertible proof of graphic photographs) would have sent him to prison, as homosexuality was not decriminalised in Britain until 1967. On top of that, he would have lost his job and the position he had worked so hard for, as well as bringing great disgrace on his family and himself.

Many answers can be found in Vassall's personality and self-image, much of it honestly revealed in his 1975 autobiography. He clearly had difficulty fitting into the British embassy in Moscow and felt in need of nurturing: 'The senior officials mostly seemed preoccupied with their own private and official duties and in some ways junior staff were left to fend for themselves. If we were cared for as one family I do not think that some of us would have got into these troubles.' As a homosexual, Vassall was an outsider in society, unable to be 'himself'. He had a social life, but one that he could not share with his colleagues. 'Being a homosexual had given me a dreadful inferiority complex', he wrote.

This was a man who had also been forced to leave a good school as a boy and give up any chance of a university education because of his family's financial circumstances. His years in the RAF were hardly welcoming to a gay man, as he himself stated. Then he was in the civil service and the closed 'old school network' must have been stifling to him. Of course, having to hide his inner feelings for years, enjoying liaisons only in secret, living a secret life – this way of life cannot have been so different from being a spy. Before being approached by the KGB, Vassall was already leading a double life (even if some obviously guessed his true sexuality), as many gay men had to at that time. This would have given him a mind able to compartmentalise, able to behave in different ways depending on whom he was with. The KGB entrapment obviously frightened and angered him, but he showed no remorse about taking money from the Russians or enjoying his affluent lifestyle in London. There may well have been a touch of revenge in Vassall's inner motivations here. Entrapped, he was spying on a society that had never accepted him for who he really was, and he was able to live a life he had only dreamed of before.

Vassall's story is one of desperation and frustration, ruthlessly capitalised on by the KGB. The Cold War was entering a new and deadlier era. It was the atomic age, and 1962 was a year when the nuclear threat would become very real. Espionage would play a hand in John F. Kennedy's eleventh-hour negotiations with the Russians during the thirteen breathless days of the Cuban Missile Crisis. And this time the double agent was not British or American.

CHAPTER 8

OLEG PENKOVSKY

The development of atomic weapons had raised the political stakes between the world's two superpowers, the United States and Soviet Russia, to a dangerous level. By the autumn of 1962, these strategic and political tensions had reached a truly frightening level. For thirteen days in October 1962, US President John F. Kennedy and Russian Premier Nikita Khrushchev played an almost fatal political and strategic chess game that would become legendary and would be known as the Cuban Missile Crisis in the West and the October Crisis in Russia.

The Cold War was entering its most deadly stage. The shooting down of the American pilot Gary Powers in a U–2 spy plane (which flew higher than any other aircraft at the time) over Russian territory in 1960 and the spy scandals that had recently rocked the West had produced a general feeling of paranoia about the East in the West and vice versa. The new power tool was to be nuclear capability and the positioning of nuclear missiles.

Cuba lay within easy missile striking distance of the United States, and by 1962 Fidel Castro was firmly in place as the communist leader of Cuba. The Americans were very wary of him, and Castro foiled many assassination attempts by the CIA, some of them truly insane, such as exploding cigars (Castro was a cigar connoisseur). The CIA even allegedly enlisted the help of the American Mafia through mobsters Johnny Roselli and Santo Trafficante (Roselli would end up dismembered, floating in an oil can in the sea off Florida, almost definitely a hit ordered by Trafficante). The United States had also funded an aborted invasion of Cuba. But by early 1962 Castro had his own plans to strike back at the United States.

In March, Castro made contact with the Russians and encouraged them to set up a missile base or bases on Cuba. His stated aim was to launch a communist revolution across Central and South America (his fellow revolutionary Che Guevara would die fighting in Bolivia five years later trying to start such a revolution there). Two months later, Khrushchev decided to take up Castro's offer and ordered the secret building of Soviet nuclear missile bases on Cuba. There were two reasons for this: to support the Cuban revolution (Khrushchev issued a statement offering support to the cause, without mentioning the setting up of nuclear bases, of course) and to gain strategic advantage over the US in the Cold War.

The positioning of Soviet nuclear bases on Cuba would become an advantage only once they were in place. The Russians were counting on the perceived sense that the Americans would not detect the building of the bases until they were operational and a de facto powerful bargaining tool. Nobody really wanted a nuclear war – the main purpose was to gain political leverage. But the Americans were sending up U-2 spy planes off the coast of America to get surveillance footage in those defensive times, and in the middle of October 1962 the footage confirmed the presence of Cuban missile bases.

A stalemate between the Americans and the Russians followed, with Khrushchev and JFK trying to outmanoeuvre each other. Kennedy held firm, and on 28 October 1962 Khrushchev announced on Radio Moscow (knowing that the Americans would be listening) that he would withdraw all Soviet missiles from Cuba. Essentially, Kennedy had won by threatening a missile strike on the Cuban bases. However, he had to promise Khrushchev during the painstaking negotiations that the US would never again fund another invasion of Cuba. By doing this, he allowed Cuba the freedom to remain a communist state (as it still is today) and – until the fall of the Soviet Union – a danger to the US as a Soviet satellite power. But nuclear war had been averted, and the Russian advantage would have been far greater if the bases had stayed on Cuba.

Kennedy had been able to keep his resolve because of the U-2 spy plane surveillance footage which showed that the Russians were not in such an advanced state of atomic capability as they liked to portray, as well as his strength of character. But that would not have been enough. He also had secret intelligence about the Russians that had enabled him to hold his position. It was intelligence gained by the CIA and the SIS of Britain, delivered by a Russian whom the CIA would later call 'the spy who saved the world'. His name was Oleg Penkovsky.

Oleg Vladimirovich Penkovsky was born in North Ossetia, Soviet Union, on 23 April 1919, just after the Russian Revolution. He came from a military family, and his father was killed fighting for the White Russians against the Bolsheviks in the civil war that followed as the communists set about moulding Russia into the new Marxist society. Oleg graduated from the Kiev Artillery Academy in 1939 at the top of his class with the officer rank of lieutenant. Showing exceptional military abilities, he was destined for a great future, and soon saw action in the Winter War against Finland and in World War Two. By the end of the war, he was a lieutenant colonel, and he joined the GRU – the Soviet Military Intelligence. He was very much an establishment figure, marrying the daughter of a general, and would later count Ivan Serov, the head of the GRU, and Chief Marshal Sergei Varentsov, the head of Soviet Strategic Rocket Forces, as close friends. Such high-level contacts would prove very useful to him.

In 1955, Oleg Penkovsky was posted to Ankara, Turkey, as a military attaché, a common cover for an intelligence agent. There are stories that Penkovsky was seen in Ankara looking lonely in cafes and bars, as if he was deeply lost in thought. His career was going from strength to strength, his future assured, yet there was something troubling him. It has been suggested that this was when the British SIS spotted him and considered him for 'turning' as a double agent. But the truth was almost definitely very different. Penkovsky was proactive in wanting to 'turn'. There are two schools of thought on this point. Most writers think that he had become increasingly disillusioned with the difference between communist ideology and the stark reality of the poverty, purges and show trials under Stalin (who was now dead) and the continuing paranoia of the regime. Others think that Penkovsky was communist to the very core and under orders to bluff the West into thinking he was dissatisfied with the Soviet system.

The truth was that Penkovsky did not need to be 'turned'. He was soon very active in offering his services to several Western intelligence agencies. After serving in Ankara he returned to Moscow and served on the Soviet Committee for Scientific Research, a prestigious posting where he had access to a great deal of secret technical material. Now a colonel, it was not long before Penkovsky made his first move. In July 1960 he approached a group of American students on

Moskvoretsky Bridge in Moscow and passed them a parcel, telling them to give it to the CIA. The CIA evaluated the material, which included enough secret data to prove that Penkovsky had access to high-grade information. However, the CIA was very sceptical that Penkovsky was a genuine defector once they had looked into his status within the GRU and his rapid promotion curve. How could such a well-connected man be a defector? They delayed in contacting Penkovsky because they knew that the KGB probably had their agents in Moscow under surveillance. There may have even been a bungled attempt at contact by a CIA agent code-named COMPASS who had a drink problem; he telephoned Penkovsky an hour later than planned, and Penkovsky could not understand his Russian anyway.

When the CIA route appeared blocked, Penkovsky did not give up. He met a Canadian businessman, Oliver Van Vleit, who was visiting Moscow from Montreal, and asked him to approach the Royal Canadian Secret Service (RCSS) on his behalf. The Canadians also turned him down, according to *The Penkovsky Papers*, published in 1965. Penkovsky must have been despairing of ever making a connection with the West. But it was third time lucky when he met Greville Wynne in Moscow. Wynne was a British businessman in charge of a trade exhibition to the Soviet Union and eastern and central Europe. But he was more than that. He had worked for MI5 during World War Two and was now in the employment of SIS, who had been recruiting British businessmen travelling overseas as part-time agents (George Blake had worked in this department of SIS shortly before; see Chapter Six). Business was a perfect cover. Wynne had the typical duties of talent spotter and contact for potential defectors or double agents, as well as acting as their courier.

Penkovsky met Wynne in Moscow in March 1961 and gave him another parcel of secret material. It is impossible to know if Wynne actively cultivated Penkovsky (Wynne would later write books highlighting his involvement), but it seems likely that Penkovsky needed little nurturing after two failed attempts to hook up with Western intelligence. As part of his job at the Soviet Committee for Scientific Research, Penkovsky had to travel abroad with an international trade delegation. Fortuitously, in April 1961 he came to London in that capacity. (This kind of lucky timing would fuel later rumours that the KGB was manoeuvring Penkovsky into position as a plant.)

By this time, SIS and the CIA had agreed to run Penkovsky jointly as an agent, and they both had officers waiting to meet him in a room at the Mount Royal Hotel in Marble Arch. The information he gave them was indeed of very high quality. Two months later, Penkovsky returned to London and met with SIS and CIA contacts again. To make Penkovsky feel welcome, the intelligence agents took photographs of him wearing both British and

American military uniforms, and these photographs of a proudly smiling Penkovsky still exist. They show a tall and slim, formal man with a military bearing.

Back in Moscow, Penkovsky and Wynne would meet many times, with Wynne acting as a courier for the documents supplied between April 1961 and July 1962, although Penkovsky also had SIS handlers, Roderick and Janet Chisholm. The material was shared jointly by SIS and the CIA, and was code-named ARNIKA. Penkovsky supplied more than 5,000 documents of high-level insider material. A CIA file declassified in March 1992 and dated 26 June 1963 reads:

> Penkovsky provided us intelligence from August 1960 through August 1962, and gave us more than 8,000 pages of translated reporting, most of which constituted highly classified Soviet defence documents.

This was an enormous amount of information in the short period of two years. But later in the memorandum the early CIA doubts about Penkovsky's authenticity are noted. It is confirmed that Penkovsky had made initial contact, but that there had been some fear that he was a Russian plant, so his 'bona fides' were checked thoroughly. The conclusion had been reached that Penkovsky was 'authentic'.

The material that Penkovsky provided was largely regarding the development of the Soviet nuclear programme. Specifically, he crucially enlightened the West that the Soviet nuclear capability was much smaller than thought before and that the missile guidance and fuelling systems were not ready to be used operationally. In *The Penkovsky Papers*, an account that was apparently made by Penkovsky himself about his espionage, then translated by a KGB defector and edited by a *Time* magazine journalist, the following remark is included: 'The Soviets have no existing means of combating enemy missiles.' The fact that the Soviet arsenal was much less sophisticated than the West had thought and that the Soviets could not defend against enemy missiles were revelations.

A late 1950s US strategy report said that the Soviet Union and satellites had more than five thousand nuclear weapons, while Penkovsky revealed that they had access to a tiny number, perhaps less than ten or twenty, and even those might not be operational. Penkovsky changed the perception of Soviet strength in the West. This knowledge was a real strategic advantage, and it is little wonder that JFK made full use of it during the tense days of the Cuban Missile Crisis, when confidence and bluff were key tactics in a game of high-stakes political poker.

But that was not all. Penkovsky also supplied details of KGB operations, Soviet politics and character assessments of Soviet leaders, as well as gossip and scandal about the ruling class. All of this information was useful to the West, but the most valuable material definitely related to strategic matters. An ex-CIA agent active in the early 1960s who was interviewed as part of *The Spying Game* programme on the History Channel shown in 1999 said: 'He was giving us a window into Soviet military planning, the philosophy behind the modernisation of the Soviet armed forces . . . a lead into where the Soviet armed forces would go for the next twenty or thirty years.'

Penkovsky was playing a dangerous game. A Russian double agent would not face a long prison sentence, as George Blake did around this time in the West, but certain death. A bullet in the back of the neck was the traditional KGB way of dealing with traitors, and an even worse fate was possible for such a high-level leak as Penkovsky. The pressure that he was under must have been enormous, but by all accounts he showed little sign of strain. He either was one hundred per cent committed to his renegade cause and resigned to the possible fatal risks or was indeed a plant used by the GRU or KGB to infiltrate the West with false information about the Soviet Union. But if he was a plant, he certainly did damage to the Soviet cause, giving the West the upper hand in facing down the Soviet nuclear threat.

Could it be that Penkovsky was a plant all along, and that Khrushchev was playing a long game? That the Cuban Missile Crisis was just an act of provocation to ensure that the United States promised never to fund an invasion of communist Cuba again? This scenario is possible but unlikely. Even if this was the Russian plan, it did not work for Khrushchev: within two years of the Soviets backing down in the Cuban Missile Crisis, he was replaced as premier, largely because of his failings on that occasion.

A CIA memorandum of 8 July 1963 from the deputy director to the director of the CIA states that a Soviet source said that it had been known for more than a year that there was a high-level intelligence leak from within the Soviet Union. The KGB began to work hard to identify the leak. It would be only matter of time before the highly effective KGB got to Penkovsky.

That day came on 22 October 1962, ironically in the middle of the Cuban Missile Crisis. Penkovsky's flat on Maxim Gorky Embankment in Moscow had been secretly searched without his knowledge in the previous month, and the KGB had found his spying equipment, supplied by SIS and the CIA, hidden in a desk with a false bottom. It is impossible to say for sure how and when the KGB apprehended him, but it is probable that he was caught while meeting a contact.

It is also possible that information given by the British double agent George Blake (see Chapter Six) had implicated Penkovsky, but this is perhaps doubtful, as Blake was arrested himself in early 1961, when Penkovsky was about to commence his spying. However, Blake may have heard about

Penkovsky's rejected approaches to the CIA and the Canadians. The KGB might have been delayed in moving in on him in case he was part of a sting operation run by the GRU on SIS and the CIA. As in Western agencies, there was inter-agency rivalry and sometimes a lack of communication. When Penkovsky was arrested, SIS and the CIA did not know that he had disappeared.

On 2 November, a call was made to a CIA officer apparently by Penkovsky (either under duress or by a KGB agent posing as him), asking for a meeting. The CIA officer duly went to the appointed rendezvous but was met by the KGB and arrested (though he was later released because of diplomatic immunity). On the very same day, Penkovsky's courier Greville Wynne was arrested in Budapest, Hungary, while on a business trip. He was taken to Moscow and held in the same prison as Penkovsky. They were both imprisoned for months, until their trial started on 7 May 1963.

Greville Wynne protested his innocence. He faced the death sentence, but from the start it was unlikely to be carried out because this was a high-profile 'show' trial, heavily reported on in the West. Wynne was sentenced to eight years in prison, some of it to be served in a labour camp, which was known to be notoriously tough. In the end he served just under a year, being released in a prisoner exchange with the Portland spy Gordon Lonsdale (aka Konon Molody). Footage of Wynne before he was released and after offers a stark comparison. He lost a great deal of weight, and his once plump face was lined and hardened by stress. He would develop an alcohol problem later and write several books and articles about his connection with Penkovsky, always putting himself in the spotlight, perhaps more than he really had been.

Oleg Penkovsky was forced to admit his guilt when presented with the evidence against him. Footage of him at the trial shows a man of great dignity under tremendous pressure. He tried to explain to the court why he had betrayed his country for the benefit of mankind. On 11 May 1963, after just four days, the court sentenced him to be shot. He was forty-four years old. It was later announced that Penkovsky was executed on 16 May 1963, but doubts have always remained as to exactly how and when it was done. Some believe that the execution never took place at all.

A CIA memorandum dated 8 July 1963 reveals the official reaction of the Soviet government to Penkovsky's exposure. According to a CIA source in Russia, 'Khrushchev mentioned in December 1962 at a gathering in Kiev . . . that Penkovsky had done a lot of harm but also that he had done some good simply on the grounds that now the United States knows the strength and technological advancement of the Soviet Union'. This sounds like political manipulation by Khrushchev, an attempt at damage limitation, since the details that the West had learnt were largely about the weakness of the Soviets' strategic nuclear capability. The memo also reports that Penkovsky's espionage had forced some minor changes in Soviet defence. That one man was able to bring about changes, however minor, in such a crucial aspect of Soviet strategy shows how damaging to the Soviet Union Penkovsky had been. But of course the main damage he inflicted was in the outcome of the Cuban Missile Crisis. By telling the CIA that Khrushchev would not be able to mobilise his meagre nuclear arsenal, Penkovsky enabled JFK to win the political chess game.

As to Penkovsky's execution, there is no definitive answer. The usual practice was to cremate the body after the person was shot. It is officially said that Penkovsky's ashes are buried in the Donskoi Monastery in Moscow. But there is a far more grisly account. In his book *Aquarium*, a Soviet defector called Vladimir Rezun claimed that he had seen an old black-and-white film at the GRU headquarters in Moscow which was apparently shown to GRU officers as an example of what happened to a Soviet traitor. Rezun wrote that in this film Penkovsky was pinned to a board with piano wire and then slowly pushed into a large furnace, feet first. This sounds very 'James Bond', but the Soviets would have been apoplectic with rage over Penkovsky's treason.

There is also the minority view that Penkovsky was never executed at all, that he was a Soviet plant from the very beginning and after the show trial and sentencing he perhaps went and lived happily in obscurity under a different name. The facts do not bear this out. Why would the Soviets want the West to know their true missile capability, especially as it was weak? This would have been a political advantage only if it were really far stronger and Penkovsky was used to lull the West into a false sense of security, with the reality revealed as a surprise tactic. This was not the case, however. Subsequent declassified material from the Soviet archives shows that the Soviet nuclear capability in 1961–62 was indeed far inferior to that of the United States, and it is probable that the Soviet Union did not have a comparable nuclear arsenal until the early 1980s.

In his book *The Second Oldest Profession*, Phillip Knightley presents another interpretation, positing that Penkovsky was a Soviet penetration plant in the beginning but then turned into a renegade and decided to rebel against the motherland. This is a possible explanation, especially in light of the clumsy and dangerous moves that Penkovsky tried to contact the West at the start, as well as his ability to travel to London to meet his intelligence contacts so quickly under the cover of a trade delegation (very much as Greville Wynne was doing the opposite way). But this theory still lacks definitive proof, like so much in the history of twentieth-century espionage.

If Penkovsky was the real deal and a bona fide

double agent, he deserves the West's gratitude. The strength, fortitude and force of conscience needed to face certain death if caught pursuing his secret actions would have been tremendous. His disillusionment and hatred of the reality of the Soviet system must have been very strong to face such risks. Apart from his discontent with the direction of his country, what other factors could have driven him into such actions? He had everything he could have wanted. He was very much part of the Soviet military and social establishment – a high-ranking, exemplary officer who had graduated at the top of his class and served with distinction in World War Two. But in that war he had been fighting the Nazis. Afterwards, Soviet foreign policy veered towards the imperialistic, although under the guise of spreading the communist revolution across Europe. Add to this the fact that Penkovsky's soldier father had died fighting the Bolsheviks decades earlier, and there was perhaps a deeply ingrained antipathy to his new masters. He was a loyal and effective servant on the outside, but perhaps his conscience was more pained as the years passed, as he saw what Stalin and his successors had done and were doing to his country. If this was the case, and it seems likely, then Oleg Penkovsky may indeed be *the* spy of the twentieth century.

In the same year that Penkovsky was probably executed, Britain was about to face the culmination of years of spy scandals – Nunn May and

Fuchs, Burgess and Maclean, the Portland Spy Ring, George Blake, John Vassall . . . The scene was now set for an affair that contained all the most lurid elements: power, sex and intrigue. And this time it would bring down a government.

CHAPTER 9

THE PROFUMO AFFAIR

On 30 July 1963, Stephen Ward took some sleeping pills to try to get some rest, as he was under an enormous amount of stress, being on trial for his part in the Profumo Affair. It was likely that Ward would be prosecuted for 'living off immoral earnings' and face imprisonment. The reputation and standing he had built up over decades lay in ruins. He knew that he was a scapegoat, and a deep sense of injustice and abandonment by his high-society friends consumed him. He was helpless in the face of the powers that be.

Apparently Ward was not alone that night. There was a freelance photojournalist with him, who was really an MI6 (SIS) officer. After Ward had gone to sleep, the man woke him up and reminded him to take some sleeping pills. Drowsy with the first dosage, Ward forgot that he had already taken some and took more. This pattern of being woken up and taking more pills was repeated until Ward, in his increasing haze, had taken enough to overdose. He slipped into a coma from which he would never awake.

Another version of the events of that night has Stephen Ward being injected with an air bubble that induced an embolism. Yet another has him poisoned. Whatever the means of causing his death, the official verdict was suicide.

The death of Dr Stephen Ward, a society osteopath with connections with powerful people, caused a tumult of headlines and media coverage. Ward was central to a scandal that had involved a Russian spy, a high-class prostitute, and the secretary of state for war, and that would in the following year contribute greatly to the bringing down of the Conservative government in Britain.

Stephen Ward was born into an ecclesiastical family, a son of the canon of Rochester Cathedral, on 19 October 1912. He went to Highgate School in north London, where the poet T. S. Eliot had taught earlier. When Stephen was seven, the family relocated to Devon when his father, Arthur, became the vicar of St Matthias Church in Torquay. But Stephen did not go to school there; instead, he was sent as a boarding pupil to the private middle-ranking Canford School in Dorset.

At Canford, Stephen was accused of attacking another pupil and was found guilty, though a teacher later said that Ward had not been responsible. The sense of injustice Stephen must have felt influenced his developing personality, and he became more independent-minded and rebellious. His father wanted him to go to university like most boys of his background, but Stephen began to veer away from this path. At the age of seventeen, he went to live in London. To support himself, he worked as a carpet salesman for a time. After a while, he moved to Hamburg in Germany and there worked as a translator for Shell Oil, as he had learnt German as a boy at school. It is probable that he visited the numerous brothels in this port town, feeding a need for sex and experimentation that would be a continuing thread throughout his life, as Anthony Summers and Stephen Dorril remarked in their 1987 book *Honeytrap: The Secret Worlds of Stephen Ward*.

Ward returned to London in 1932 and once again became a salesman, selling Indian tea and signing up subscribers for the *Spectator* magazine. Now twenty years old, he had become a confident and enthusiastically urbane young man with very good conversation skills that would serve him well in his later career. He might easily have remained a salesman, perhaps setting up his own business, as he certainly had the ability. But his mother was not pleased with the lack of structure in his life, and she wanted him to learn a profession if he was not going to university. She convinced him to train in osteopathy, the treatment of pain and stiffness in joints, muscles and bones. To do this, he was to go to study in the United States – probably because to study osteopathy in Britain he would have needed a medical degree.

Ward left for the US in 1934 and attended the Kirksville College of Osteopathy and Surgery in Missouri. He received good training in osteopathy there, but much of his time was taken up with dealing with more general medical procedures, such as treating the victims of natural disasters and helping to deliver babies. This must have been a harsh baptism to the world, but Ward seems to have coped very well. He had a great love of the United States which would remain with him for the rest of his life. He particularly liked the openness of the American attitude, as opposed to the reserved, somewhat austere attitude of the British. He would return to Britain as a trained osteopath and a worldly man.

In 1940, at the age of twenty-seven, Ward started his own osteopathy practice back in Torquay, Devon. His client base began to build, but World War Two intervened. In 1941 he offered his services to the Royal Army Medical Corps, but even in wartime he was turned down because this elite medical section of the British army did not recognise his American osteopathy qualification. However, the Royal Armoured Corps soon accepted him, and he began to treat injured officers. He showed a natural talent not only for the medical component of the job but also for the social aspect. His calm and personable character was popular with patients. But bureaucracy once again intervened. A Royal Army Medical Corps officer attached to the Royal Armoured Corps complained that Ward was not using accepted methods in his osteopathy treatments. Astonishingly, Ward faced a court martial and ended up as a stretcher-bearer in the Royal Army Medical Corps. Not surprisingly, especially given his independent character, he was furious. Ward was something of a maverick by nature, and following the established rules and submitting to authority were not his strong points.

In March 1944 Ward was posted to India with the army. Incredibly, one of his patients there was Mahatma Gandhi, whom he treated for neck pain and headaches. He was very impressed with Gandhi and recognised the peace leader's aura of greatness. This ability to gain access to important people was characteristic of Stephen Ward. He was an opportunist who shrewdly knew how to get what he wanted socially. Status and prestige were important to him, and many of his actions were geared towards achieving these objectives.

At the end of the war, Ward returned to Britain and worked for the Osteopathic Association Clinic in Dorset Square, central London. It is said by several sources that when a private client rang the clinic and requested the services of 'the best osteopath in London', Ward recommended himself. He was not short of confidence, and his opportunism paid dividends, providing the break into the London and Hollywood high society that he craved. In this insular high echelon, word of mouth was very powerful. Within a couple of years,

Stephen Ward was treating Winston Churchill and other political luminaries, as well as the Hollywood actors Ava Gardner and Mel Ferrer. By building this impressive client base, Ward was able to start his own osteopathy practice in Cavendish Square, just behind the prestigious Selfridges department store and very close to the famous London medical centres of Harley Street and Wimpole Street. His client list was ever growing and he was also making acquaintances through his patients, being invited to play bridge (Ward was a good player) and to dinner parties.

Something of a gadfly, Ward was mixing with film starlets such as Celia Lipton (there is a photograph of Ward attending a film premiere with her in 1948) and, later, Maureen Swanson. Style and image were important to him. With his perfectly slicked back and pomaded hair, sharp suits, elegant manner and relaxed social grace, he had morphed into what he had always wanted to be. Beautiful women were often seen on his arm, and on 27 July 1948, he married a fashion model, Patricia Baines, at Marylebone Registry Office, a short walk from his flat and clinic. The relationship did not last – she moved out of his flat after a month and a half. It is not difficult to understand why: Ward was spontaneous, impulsive and perhaps somewhat shallow. Commitment was not his strong suit. During these years, Ward was regularly drinking with Prince Philip, soon to be the Queen's consort, and other aristocratic men such as the Marquis of Milford Haven. He drove a gleaming white Jaguar, and a photograph shows him nonchalantly leaning on its running board.

Ward was also putting his drawing skills to good use. He was a fine artist, and could have gone fully professional (he did in fact win many commissions and carried them out alongside his osteopathic work). Among many others, Ward drew Prime Minister Harold Macmillan, Chancellor of the Exchequer Selwyn Lloyd, Sir Winston Churchill, Labour leader Hugh Gaitskell and actor Douglas Fairbanks Jr. By the late 1950s, his social circle ranged from the truly prestigious and powerful to the seedy and infamous. As well as being on friendly terms with newspaper editor Colin Coote and with Roger Hollis, the head of MI5, he knew well the infamous slum landlord Peter Rachman. Ward's contact book must have looked like a who's who of elite London society, but there was a much seamier side to his life as well.

Ward's high sex drive and the need to attract women remained unabated. Very attractive young girls, usually in their late teens and early twenties, surrounded him. Some of them stayed for long periods at his flat in Wimpole Mews after he moved there from Cavendish Square. Most prominent among these young women were Mandy Rice-Davies, an 'ex-girlfriend' of Peter Rachman, and Christine Keeler. Keeler was a real beauty, tall and slim, with dark chestnut hair, shining brown eyes and flawless porcelain skin.

She was to play a pivotal role in the scandal that would ensue and lead to Ward's downfall.

Christine Keeler was born in Uxbridge in Middlesex on 22 February 1942, but she spent most of her childhood living in two converted train carriages in a village in Berkshire with her mother and stepfather. This unconventional childhood was cut short when Christine, at the age of fifteen, was offered a job as a model for a dress shop in Soho in London (living models were quite common then in high-class shops). The following year, 1958, she became pregnant by an African-American army sergeant based in the UK. The soldier went back to the US before Christine found out that she was pregnant. She returned to her mother and stepfather and tried to abort the baby herself but was unsuccessful. The baby was premature and was born sickly in April 1959, living for only six days.

Returning to London, Keeler worked as a waitress in Baker Street and struck up a conversation there with a young woman who worked as a topless showgirl at Murray's Cabaret Club in Soho, then heaving with vice, both legal and illegal. The club's owner hired Christine to do the same job, and one of the patrons turned out to be Dr Stephen Ward, the society osteopath. Pieces of a fatal jigsaw were now beginning to fall into place. Christine Keeler soon moved into Ward's Wimpole Mews flat, but she always maintained that there was no sexual relationship between them.

Accusations would later be made against Stephen Ward that he was effectively a pimp, supplying attractive young women to his wealthy and aristocratic friends. Muriel Jakubait and Monica Weller, authors of *Ruth Ellis: My Sister's Secret Life*, even claimed that Ruth Ellis, a society club hostess and the last woman to be hanged in Britain in 1955 (for shooting her lover), was 'run' by Ward. There is no doubt that Ward introduced young women such as Christine Keeler and Mandy Rice-Davies to society acquaintances, but no firm evidence exists that he was profiting financially from these introductions. As well, not all of his beauties were hostesses, dancers and showgirls; various film stars and the future international model Maggie Brown were also in his orbit. As Ward said himself, he took some rent from the girls who lived in his flat, but that is different from living off of immoral earnings, a criminal offence. However, there is no doubt that Ward's ability to hook up powerful men with beautiful women enhanced his status socially and helped make him one of the inner circle. This was Ward the player, schmoozer and middleman. Just as his osteopathic and drawing skills and easy social charm had gained him initial entry into the height of London society, his aptitude for such introductions was definitely a factor in ingratiating him further to those with the power and glamour he so sought.

By the late 1950s and continuing into the 1960s, Ward had access to a cottage on the vast Cliveden estate in Buckinghamshire, owned by Lord Astor, a good friend. Ward would visit Spring Cottage on most weekends, and many of the girls he knew joined him there. There is a photograph of Maggie Brown with Ward on a sofa at the cottage. The photo was taken by a Russian acquaintance, Captain Yevgeny (Eugene) Ivanov, an assistant naval attaché at the Soviet embassy in London, sometime in the early 1960s.

Ward and Ivanov had met at a lunch at the Garrick Club in London in January 1961, introduced by the managing editor of *The Daily Telegraph* newspaper, Captain Colin Coote. Coote had worked for SIS after World War One and had many intelligence connections. He had first met Ward when the latter treated him for his bad back. When the treatment was successful, Coote invited Ward to his house to play bridge and they became friends. At one point, Ward apparently told Coote that he wanted to visit Moscow to try to draw Khrushchev but that he would have problems getting a visa (although Ward later denied saying this). In his memoirs (which according to the writers Anthony Summers and Stephen Dorril are riddled with inaccuracies), Coote said that he introduced Ward to Ivanov as a favour to help with a visa; he had recently met Ivanov shortly before, when a group of Russian naval officers had visited *The Daily Telegraph* offices on a tour. Ward and Ivanov became friendly, and that is when Ivanov began to visit the Cliveden cottage.

In 1961, Ivanov was thirty-five years old and a

rising star in Soviet intelligence. He was an attaché outwardly, but this was a common cover for intelligence agents. According to an MI5 source, it is possible that Ivanov had been sent to London to control the Portland Spy Ring, the members of which were arrested in January 1961. Ivanov was a social animal, and it is certain that part of his remit in London was to try to penetrate high society and pick up any gossip and information he could. He was handsome, athletic and attractive to women, and he possessed elegant social skills. Nevertheless, many society people with whom he came into contact were initially suspicious of him being a Russian – the Cold War was in full swing. Even when they did get to know him, there was a large element of tokenism in their acceptance of him: a real live Russian in their midst! Ward was amiable with Ivanov; he did not have communist leanings, but he saw the Russians as human beings, and his open-mindedness was no doubt a result of his earlier wide travels. Ivanov had to follow the rules of the Soviet embassy and ask permission to travel outside of a twenty-five mile radius of London, but Spring Cottage was just within that periphery. He was a visitor there on many occasions, and he mixed socially with all members of Ward's circle, including Christine Keeler and Lord Astor.

The fact is that MI5 had already identified Ivanov as a Soviet intelligence agent. Could it have been possible that MI5 asked Coote, with his intelligence connections, to set up the meeting with Ward? Was MI5 trying to turn Ivanov, with Ward as the pawn? There is no strong proof that MI5 were playing Ward at this stage, but they probably did so later, when they saw that Ivanov was relaxed and enjoying Ward's hospitality. There are photographs (with the heads cut off) of society people in Ward's circle having an orgy during this period. Did MI5 want to take compromising photographs of Ivanov in such a situation, just as the KGB had set up John Vassall (see Chapter Eight) six years earlier? Was it truly an MI5 honey-trap operation? All of these questions are valid and have been asked but not conclusively answered.

To complicate matters, there was also a connection with President John F. Kennedy. In June 1961, Kennedy arrived in London for political talks with British Prime Minister Harold Macmillan. Kennedy had come directly from Moscow, where he had held a summit with Russian Premier Khrushchev, a tenuous political relationship that would later culminate in the Cuban Missile Crisis (see Chapter Eight). Kennedy suffered from an excruciatingly bad back and Addison's disease (both kept secret from the US electorate). The former had recently been aggravated when he strained his back at a cere-monial tree planting. During his London visit, back specialists treated Kennedy, and it has been alleged by Anthony Summers in his book *Honeytrap* that one of them was none other than

Stephen Ward (Ward had earlier treated President Eisenhower on a London trip). But that was not the only connection. An FBI memo of 27 August 1963 shows that the FBI were worried about Kennedy's connection to two women associated with Stephen Ward. Some parts of the memo have been blanked out, but there is enough there to show that fear. We now know that JFK had an abnormally strong sex drive, and it is said that he told a shocked Macmillan on that trip that he got a headache if he went too long without sex. There is little wonder that the FBI were concerned. If this connection had been exposed, Kennedy would also have been embroiled in the Profumo scandal that followed.

Events were moving forward for Stephen Ward, but not of his own making. On 8 June 1961, Ward took a phone call from the War Office, asking him casually to meet a 'Mr Woods' for a chat. As Anthony Summers and Stephen Dorril uncovered in their book *Honeytrap*, 'Mr Woods' was really the MI5 counter-intelligence officer Keith Wagstaffe. They met in Marylebone High Street, and Wagstaffe asked Ward about his friendship with Eugene Ivanov. Ward asked if it was a problem, and Wagstaffe said that it was not, but that he would appreciate it if Ward got in touch if Ivanov should ask any strange or searching questions. We now know that MI5's suspicions about Ivanov were probably correct, as Ivanov wrote to Christine Keeler many years later and apologised for using her to try to get information, as Keeler wrote in her memoirs. Ward was only too happy to be of assistance, and promised to help if he could. It can be imagined how this intrigue appealed to Ward's need for glamour and adventure, especially in the same year that the Portland Spy Ring and George Blake were all over the newspapers and the first James Bond film was being filmed. Spying had never been more in the public eye.

Ward took Wagstaffe back to his Wimpole Mews flat, where Wagstaffe saw Christine Keeler, who was living there. Wagstaffe later commented about how beautiful she was, if somewhat provocatively dressed. Could he have reported this to MI5 and the agency decided to use Keeler through Ward as a honeytrap for Ivanov? Was Ward being used as an MI5 agent? Not at this stage, but he was certainly asked to supply any information that came his way from Ivanov.

Ivanov was aware that he was vulnerable, and he was too shrewd an operator to fall into this trap: he had even told Ward earlier that MI5 would contact him regarding their friendship. But Keith Wagstaffe's opinion of Ward in his official MI5 report confirms what we know about the osteopath. Wagstaffe found him charming and personable and noted he had some left-leaning ideas that the Russians could have taken advantage of. Basically, Wagstaffe did not consider Ward a security risk but also did not think that he should be used as an agent. But that was the official version. Was Ward really being manoeuvred to set up Ivanov? Ward's contacts and the circles in which he moved would have been a perfect cover for him. As with the Cambridge spy Guy Burgess (see Chapter Three), Ward's sociable personality and playboy lifestyle made him seem an unlikely spy. Ward would never be a man in the shadows.

The relationship between Ward the society osteopath and the covert Russian intelligence officer Ivanov would form the foundation of the scandal that was to follow. Added to this was the presence of the delectable Christine Keeler at many Cliveden gatherings. Only one more piece of the jigsaw was required to complete the puzzle now.

John Profumo was the minister for war in Harold Macmillan's Conservative government, a very sensitive and crucial diplomatic position, controlling the entire War Office. Born on 30 January 1915 in London, Profumo was the son of Baron Albert Profumo, a barrister and diplomat of Italian blood (John decided not to use the title when his father died in 1940). John Profumo attended the elite Harrow School followed by Oxford University, and at the latter he was a member of the notorious Bullingdon Club, a selective social grouping of well-heeled young men that continues to this day. It would be hard to imagine a much more privileged and establishment

British background. The family had both title and wealth, along with the attendant connections.

John Profumo joined the army in 1939 at the outbreak of World War Two and served with some distinction (he was mentioned in dispatches). He served in North Africa, at the D-Day landings in France and in Italy, for this last receiving an Order of the British Empire (OBE) for his military contribution. In 1940, the year that his father died and whilst still in the army, Profumo was elected as the Conservative MP for Kettering, Northamptonshire, in Neville Chamberlain's government. It was not so uncommon then for MPs to be actively serving in the forces during the war, and it was popular among voters. Profumo had all the credentials: intelligence, impeccable background, education and connections, personality and charm. He could so easily have sat back in Parliament and coasted, but he soon showed himself to be ambitious and independent-minded. Very soon after taking his seat as an MP, Profumo broke ranks and voted against his own party on a matter of principle in a key debate in Parliament. This upset some of his colleagues, especially the Conservative government whip, whose job it was to keep the Conservative MPs in line. The whip wrote to Profumo and called him an 'utterly contemptible little shit' for voting against his own party.

It was this independence of spirit that served Profumo well in the army and in his civilian career.

Although he lost his Kettering parliamentary seat in 1945, he would return again and rise fast. His connections got him the post of the chief of the British Mission to Japan, and on leaving the army in 1950, having risen to the rank of brigadier, he was elected as an MP for Stratford-upon-Avon in Warwickshire (Shakespeare's birthplace). The Conservative Party had been out of power in his absence, but when they formed the government again in 1951 Profumo began his ascendancy. He would hold key senior positions over the next seven years, in the ministries of Civil Aviation, Transport, Colonies and Foreign Office, before becoming minister of state for foreign affairs in 1959. The following year, he was made the minister for war, although he did not sit in the Cabinet. This role was crucial, especially as the Cold War was just entering its most dangerous phase.

In 1954 Profumo had married the famous actress Valerie Hobson. Beautiful, sophisticated and elegant, she was a good wife as well as being a great political asset. They soon had children, and John Profumo's image as the brilliant young rising politician and secure family man was established. But like many politicians, Profumo had a fatal flaw: his taste for beautiful women. And for that he would risk everything he had achieved.

It is not difficult to see how John Profumo came to mix in the same circles as Stephen Ward, and with Ward there were always beautiful women. It was in July 1961, when Profumo had been the minister for war for a year, that he attended a party on Lord Astor's Cliveden estate (Profumo's wife was also there). Legend has it that at the party Profumo saw Christine Keeler, aged nineteen, emerging naked from the swimming pool, grasping for a towel. She transfixed him, and there could have been only one outcome: Profumo was soon having an affair with Keeler. Profumo's son, David, in his 2006 memoir about his father titled *Bringing the House Down* states that his father had told him that he had probably met Keeler previously at Murray's, a London club. Whatever the truth, unknown to John Profumo, Keeler was probably also having an affair with the Soviet attaché Eugene Ivanov.

If MI5 were really trying to trap Ivanov through Ward, the link with John Profumo would have been greatly unwelcome. His sensitive political position complicated matters a great deal. Profumo would have been as discreet as he could, but MI5 were keeping close tabs on Ivanov and Ward, so they must have found out about his relationship with Keeler. But the explosive part was Profumo's indirect connection, through Keeler, with Ivanov. Whether Ward was being manipulated by MI5 to entrap Ivanov or not, a perfect MI5 honeytrap was rapidly gaining potential for a huge scandal.

John Profumo kept the affair with Keeler going for only a few weeks, as rumours about it were beginning to spread in society circles. Sir Norman

Brook, the cabinet secretary, was approached by the MI5 chief Sir Roger Hollis (himself later accused of being a KGB double agent), who asked him to speak to Profumo. Brook did just that, and on 9 August 1961 Profumo wrote to Keeler, ending the affair. It could have all died there and been no more than a secret case of adultery, if two other men who had connections with Christine Keeler had not had a fight in public over her which involved shooting. The newspapers began to focus on Keeler because of this affray and after some digging they soon uncovered her connections to both Profumo and Ivanov. This was of course exclusive dynamite for them, but the libel laws and the more respectful treatment of politicians in the early 1960s by the media prevented them from publishing their discovering. But just as the suspicions about Kim Philby's treachery became public through Parliament (see Chapter Three), so did the Profumo-Keeler-Ivanov connection.

In March 1963 the Labour MP George Wigg, probably for political party motives as much as for reasons of national security, referred to the rumours that John Profumo had had an affair with Keeler. (He could make such claims freely as Parliament is exempt from the libel laws within the House of Commons.) This forced Profumo to make a statement to Parliament that there had never been 'any impropriety' between him and Keeler. Profumo had little choice in the circumstances if he wanted to hold off the scandal. But it was this very denial that would prove to be his undoing.

The fact that Profumo had denied any involvement with Keeler should have silenced the media to a large extent, especially as Profumo had threatened legal action if any allegations against him were printed. But over the following three months the national newspapers continued to publish articles about Christine Keeler. Most of them were largely insinuations, but this kept the story in the public eye. The salacious details of a possible sex scandal between a government minister, Profumo, and Keeler, described as a 'high-class call girl', was dangerous enough for Macmillan's government. The added element of Keeler's connection to Eugene Ivanov lifted the affair into another dimension in the wake of the Blake and Vassall spy cases. This was exacerbated further in 1963 when Kim Philby fled to Moscow and was finally confirmed as 'the Third Man' in the Cambridge spy ring. Cold War tensions in the aftermath of the Cuban Missile Crisis were at a height, and the timing for Macmillan's government could not have been worse. It is possible that that this was the Soviet plan all along – to destabilise the Conservative government by using Ivanov, as a Labour government would be more conducive to Soviet interests. However, this is a very tenuous argument, as Profumo's connection with Keeler was an accident of circumstance, and any suggestion that Stephen Ward was in the pay of the Russians to set up the meeting has no evidential foundation.

The former high-ranking MI5 officer Peter Wright claimed in his book *Spycatcher* that when he interviewed Keeler as a counter-intelligence officer, he found her poorly educated and uninformed. Yet during the course of the discussion she mentioned a term used in nuclear circles at the time that was not in common use. This could have meant that Ivanov was trying to get information through Keeler from Profumo. This is possible, especially since Ivanov wrote to Keeler years later apologising for using her to get information, as already mentioned. Could Stephen Ward also have been involved? While not impossible, this is extremely unlikely.

Christine Keeler was now something of a notorious celebrity, and when she posed naked for the photographer Lewis Morley in May 1963, sitting on a wooden high-backed chair and showing nothing but insinuating a great deal, her infamy increased tenfold. A copy of the photograph was stolen and published in the *Sunday Mirror*, then in many other newspapers. This has become the iconic image of the Profumo affair, synonymous with the scandal – with the young Keeler's seductive beauty crystallised forever. The playwright Joe Orton replicated the pose just a few years later for a famous photograph published in a magazine.

The Profumo affair is now a cultural landmark of 1960s Britain, and the photograph is intrinsic to its continued existence in popular culture.

The pressure was mounting on Profumo, with gossip quickly diminishing his chances of political survival. Profumo confessed his guilt over the affair to his wife, and Valerie loyally promised to stand by him. To belatedly limit the damage to the Conservative government, Profumo duly admitted to lying to the House of Commons. This was a very serious offence in Parliament, and still is now. His resignation was inevitable, and it followed on 5 June 1963.

Prime Minister Harold Macmillan then had to order an inquiry into the affair, and Lord Denning was put in charge of it. Meanwhile, soon after Profumo's resignation, Eugene Ivanov was recalled back to Moscow – and so swiftly disappeared from the London scene. The Soviets obviously did not want to risk Ivanov being arrested or the bad publicity of him being expelled under diplomatic immunity. The finger of the law now had to point at one of the other key players of the affair: Stephen Ward.

Ward had continued to practise as an osteopath, but the growing storm had not left him untouched. He outwardly continued his life, but the pressure on him was immense. Shortly after Profumo resigned, Ward was arrested and taken to Marylebone Lane police station. The charge against him was that he had been acting as a procurer of women for sexual favours: 'That he, being a man, did on divers [sic] dates between January 1961 and 8 June 1963, knowingly live wholly or in part on the earning of prostitution . . . contrary to the Sexual Offences Act 1956.' This would ruin Ward, and he knew it. Society then was far more judgemental in such matters than it is now. The police were gathering 'evidence' against Ward, and two prostitutes named Ronna Ricardo and Vickie Barret were interviewed. Ricardo and Barret both accused Ward of acting as a procurer (basically a pimp), and these claims were added to his charge sheet.

The trial of Stephen Ward began at the Old Bailey on 22 July 1963. The charges brought on the evidence of Ricardo and Barret were broken down in court, with Ricardo taking back her allegations against Ward, and with Barret's evidence found to be unreliable in a legal sense. Christine Keeler and Mandy Rice-Davies were also called as witnesses. The prosecuting counsel, Mervin Griffith-Jones, launched a scathing character attack on Ward in his closing speech, and it was on the night of that speech that Ward apparently took an overdose – or rather, was murdered or assisted in dying. The next morning Stephen Ward was in a coma, but the judge ordered that the trial should continue, and the jury was sent out to reach their verdict. On 31 July, the verdict came in, finding Ward guilty of 'living off the immoral earnings' of Keeler and Rice-Davies, but not guilty of the more serious charges of pimping. The judge then adjourned the court until Ward could attend the sentencing. On 3 August, Ward died in hospital without ever waking from his coma. Two days later, the case was closed.

Lord Denning's official inquiry into the affair, which became known as 'The Denning Report' was published on 25 September 1963. It was a notable report in that it was the first time that the public learnt that the officially non-existent MI5 was responsible to the Home Secretary. But apart from that revelation, there was little new evidence. Denning's conclusion was that there had been no security leak because of the Profumo-Keeler-Ivanov connection. The report also stated that there was no MI5 involvement (which we now know is very unlikely), and Denning saw the events as a series of unfortunate coincidences. Stephen Ward was the scapegoat in the report: much of the blame was put on him. This was convenient, as of course he was dead. But as Summers and Dorril state in their book *Honeytrap*, 'the evidence bears the fingerprints of British Intelligence, manoeuvring against Soviet Intelligence, groping to please its counterparts at the CIA'. The point about the CIA is especially important, as the CIA's confidence in British Intelligence had been greatly damaged by the Cambridge spies, Portland spies, Fuchs, Blake and Vassall.

Less than a month after the report was published, Harold Macmillan resigned because of ill health, the stress of the Profumo affair greatly contributing to this decision. Foreign Secretary Alec Douglas-Home succeeded him. The Conservative government was roundly defeated in the general election of 1964, with Harold Wilson becoming the new Labour prime minister. It is widely agreed that the Profumo affair was a key factor in this defeat, along with the changes in popular culture. The affair had done a great deal to emphasise what was wrong with the 'old' establishment (although many vestiges of it still remain to this day). Never before or since has an espionage scandal had such an impact on the public consciousness and such political repercussions.

After the scandal, John Profumo withdrew from public life and became a charity worker and then a fundraiser for the underprivileged at Toynbee Hall in east London. He was not paid for this work, but his family had private wealth. He redeemed himself in the eyes of many, and in 1975 the Queen made him a Commander of the British Empire (CBE) for his charity work. In 2003 he was given a major charity prize, the Beacon Fellowship Prize. In the last years of his life he appeared in public more, attending official dinners and memorial services. He died of a stroke on 7 March 2006. His obituaries were largely positive, focusing on his charity work, but his name will forever be synonymous with the scandal.

Christine Keeler has resurfaced in the public

consciousness from time to time, and she has written several books about her role in the Profumo affair, some of them making sensational unsupported claims. The Kremlin did not give Eugene Ivanov much recognition in Moscow, and his wife left him over his brief relationship with Keeler. Ivanov became a heavy drinker, and he famously had dinner with Keeler in Moscow in 1993. He died on 17 January 1994.

Of course, the other major player in the affair, Stephen Ward, had died over thirty years earlier. It does seem that Ward was used by MI5 to try to trap Ivanov through Keeler, and the involvement of John Profumo was a very unfortunate development for him. There is no evidence whatsoever that Ward instigated the affair between Keeler and Profumo for any sinister motive. Ward was ruined by the trial, but would he have committed suicide, as the official verdict decided? It was certainly convenient for the powers that be that he died when he did. Ward was a victim of his own naivety and craving for social advancement and status. He became a pawn in a dangerous game, and circumstances found him drowning in political currents far too strong for him to swim against.

The Profumo affair was the last big British spy scandal of the twentieth century. After a string of espionage controversies, recruitment methods and vetting procedures were tightened up. The Cold War would continue to bring mysterious deaths, such as that of the communist dissident Georgi Markov, poisoned by an umbrella tip in London in 1978, probably on KGB orders. But a spying scandal would never strike at the heart of the British establishment in the same way again, at least not any we know about. However, across the Atlantic, the CIA would have their own problems, which would run right into the 1990s.

CHAPTER 10

ALDRICH AMES

On 21 February 1994, an expensive Jaguar was being driven through the capital and political powerbase of the United States, Washington, DC. All of a sudden another car forced it to the side of the road, and several dark-suited FBI agents jumped out of the other car. The tall middle-aged man wearing glasses at the wheel of the Jaguar was ordered to get out and place his hands on the Jaguar's roof. The man's name was Aldrich Ames, and he had been an active CIA agent for twenty-five years. Ames remained calm when he was arrested for espionage against the United States.

'Espionage, me – you've got to be kidding!' he said before being bundled into the back of the FBI vehicle and driven to FBI headquarters. On the way, a message came over the car radio stating that Ames's home was going to be searched. When he heard this, Ames lowered his head and swore under his breath. His Colombian wife, Rosario, was also arrested that day.

It soon became clear why Ames did not want his home searched. In his garage the FBI found a bounty of evidence proving his espionage for the Russians. Special agents found bags of CIA files and computer discs which should not have left the CIA's premises, along with bank statements showing numerous payments made to Ames by the KGB and its successor agency. Ames later admitted in an interview from prison for *The Spying Game* programme first broadcast on the History Channel in 1999: 'I am a careless person. I was quite sloppy in the way I handled my security.'

Aldrich and Rosario Ames were both charged with spying for the Soviet Union and then Russia. After a trial, Ames was sentenced to life for espionage and his wife to five years for conspiracy to commit espionage and for tax evasion. At the end of her sentence, Rosario Ames was deported back to Colombia. At the time of writing, Aldrich Ames was serving his life sentence at the United States Penitentiary in Allenwood, Pennsylvania. He was lucky to escape the death penalty.

It is estimated that Aldrich Ames betrayed over a hundred CIA operations to the Russians, as well as blowing the covers of at least thirty Western intelligence agents. On top of this, many Russian CIA contacts or 'assets' were executed as a result of his treachery. The CIA had overlooked the signs of Ames being a double agent, but the FBI had been on to him for some time. He was not the only CIA or FBI agent to be exposed as a Russian spy at the end of the twentieth century. Other notable traitors include the FBI agent Robert Hanssen, who spied for the Russians for over fifteen years, and Harold Nicholson, a senior CIA agent who started spying for the Russians in the year that Ames was arrested. But Aldrich Ames is regarded as the most damaging because of the scale of his treachery, and his motivations for turning double agent illustrate a different kind of spy.

Aldrich Hazen Ames was born on 26 May 1941 in River Falls, Wisconsin. He went to McLean High School in McLean, Virginia, before starting work for the CIA in 1962 in a low-level administrative job as a document analyst. This was purely a financial move to help pay for his university years, and Ames later said that he had had no great CIA career plan at that point. But after he graduated from George Washington University with a BA in History in September 1967, he remained at the CIA, earning promotion to the Records Integration Division of the Operations Directorate, the beating heart of CIA operations. He was accepted into the Career Trainee Program in December 1967. The CIA Inspector General's report on the Ames case from October 1994 states that Ames had shown a particular fascination with operations against communist countries. The CIA enrolled him in a Turkish language course.

In 1969, at the age of twenty-seven, Ames became a fully-fledged CIA case officer and was posted to Ankara in Turkey. It was normal procedure to send a new officer out into the field, and Ames's remit was to try to recruit Soviet intelligence officers to work secretly for the CIA. Ames did manage to infiltrate a communist organisation in Ankara through a close friend of a student activist after paying for a list of the activist's contacts (the activist, Deniz Gezmi?, was later executed). Ames remained in Turkey until 1972, but his first 'tour of duty' was not considered a success. His last appraisal in Turkey states that he was not suited for fieldwork. Field intelligence agents must possess guile and the ability to manipulate contacts and situations, and it was written that Ames would rather have assignments that 'do not involve face-to-face situations with relatively unknown personalities who must be manipulated'. When Ames saw his appraisal, he considered leaving the CIA.

He remained, however, and for the following four years was based at Langley, the CIA headquarters in Virginia, in the Soviet-East Europe (SE) Division. In this role, he helped plan operations, and he was far more successful as a desk officer, with supervisors praising his work. He became so valued that in September 1974 he was assigned to manage the case of a valuable CIA 'asset', the Soviet diplomat Aleksandr Ogorodnik. Ames had also married by this time, to co-worker Nancy Segebarth, but the relationship was not a happy one. During these years, Ames began to drink heavily, often venturing on sprees to avoid going home.

It was CIA policy to rotate agents, and in 1976 Ames was posted to the Foreign Resources Division in New York. He continued to do well there and was recommended for promotion. In 1981 he was posted to Mexico City and in May 1982 he was duly promoted. In Mexico, however, Ames did not thrive. At CIA headquarters and in New York, he had been dealing with established sources and assets, but now had to discover and develop new ones, as earlier in Turkey. His drinking got worse, probably in some part due to the pressure he was under, and his work and financial accountings were found lacking. He was also involved in an adulterous affair (he was still married to Nancy) with a Colombian embassy cultural attaché, Maria del Rosario Casas Dupuy, who was to feature significantly in Ames's future. His appraisals in Mexico City were generally negative, and in 1983 he was back at CIA headquarters.

On his return, Ames was not demoted but given a responsible position as chief of a section of the SE Division, where he had access to global CIA anti-Soviet operations. He began divorce proceedings against Nancy and started living with Maria del Rosario Casas Dupuy – usually referred to as Rosario – whom he would soon marry. The financial pressure of the divorce settlement and Rosario's taste for shopping put a further financial strain on Ames. Ames was already in severe debt, with a developing alcohol problem, and although he was on a good salary, he lived beyond his means. With his newly gained access to highly classified global CIA assets, he began to see a way to make some desperately needed money. On 16 April 1985, Ames walked into the Soviet embassy in Washington, DC, and offered secrets for cash. Such a 'walk-in' must have made the Soviet embassy staff very suspicious, but after they checked him out the stage was set for Ames to become a double agent. Ames explained in *The Spying Game* interview in 1999: 'My little scam in April 1985 went like this – give me $50,000; here's some names of people we've recruited.' On 17 May, he met a contact for lunch, but at these first two meetings he gave over little of value. That would soon change.

On 13 June, Ames went into the Chadwicks diner in Georgetown, a waterfront area of Washington. It was a busy restaurant, and Ames sat with a Russian man in a wooden booth. The man was Sergey D. Chuvakhin, a Soviet diplomat. After they chatted over lunch, Ames passed Chuvakhin a bag full of highly classified CIA documents. In those files were the identities of almost all of the Russian spies being run by the CIA. Ames later remarked: 'The only thing I ever withheld from the KGB were the names of two agents whom I personally had known and handled and had a particular feeling for.'

Ames has always claimed that it was a purely financial motivation that made him go to the meeting at the diner, but as Milton Bearden and James Risen point out in their book *The Main Enemy*, there may have been another trigger too. Ames had already compromised himself by walking into the Soviet embassy, and just over three weeks before the meeting at Chadwicks, the FBI had arrested John Walker, the leader of a Soviet spy ring in the US Navy. Publicly, it was said that Walker's wife had shopped him to the FBI, but Ames may well have believed that the KGB had betrayed Walker and might do the same to him. Since he had already provided enough information to put himself at risk, he might as well benefit financially by going through with his proposition. Once he had taken this step into treachery, he did not look back, and he continued to supply information in return for large amounts of money.

In 1986, Ames was transferred to Rome, where he was made chief of a section dealing with CIA operations in Italy. His work performance was lacklustre there, and he drank heavily, although he did perform his liaison role with US Military Intelligence adequately. When the branch he ran was closed down in a reorganisation in December 1989, he was made the chief of another SE Division section in Rome, where he stayed until October 1990. His appraisal at this time ranked him in the bottom ten per cent of officers of his rank, largely due to his lack of attention to detail, uncouth drinking habits and poor administrative performance. Back at CIA headquarters, Ames was moved to a position in the Counterintelligence Center (CIC). His job was to analyse and write reports on the KGB. He remained in that post until August 1991, when he returned briefly to SE Division. Then, in December 1991, he was moved to work in the Counternarcotics Program (CNC).

Over nearly nine years, Ames betrayed numerous CIA operations to the Soviets, with many Russian double agents disappearing. Perhaps the highest-profile person betrayed by him was Colonel Oleg Gordievsky, who was the head of the Soviet intelligence gathering unit in London and who was being run by the British SIS (MI6) as a double agent. Luckily for Gordievsky, he was rescued from Moscow, where he had returned just before the KGB arrested him (his fate probably would have been death). Ames himself later said in *The Spying Game* interview from prison that he admired this SIS operation: 'I was one of many in the Agency who really applauded and admired the SIS's skill and commitment to getting him [Gordievsky] out. We thought it was terrific. I did too.'

But the Gordievsky betrayal was one in a long list of Western intelligence assets whose covers were blown, and it was obvious that there was a mole. The source of a leak was slowly narrowed down to the CIA. The fact that Ames was now visibly living way beyond the means of his CIA salary helped pinpoint him. In 1991, the FBI began a huge surveillance operation against suspects, and Ames had his home and car bugged. FBI operatives sifted through the rubbish bins outside his house and found the ripped-up draft of a note Ames was planning to pass to the KGB at a dead letter drop. The FBI patiently built up the evidence against him until they had enough to arrest him for espionage. Ames was finally arrested on 21 February 1994. He was due to fly to Moscow the very next day on CIA business, and the FBI may have been worried that he would never return.

Why did the CIA not investigate and arrest Ames itself, especially as relations between the CIA and FBI have always been competitive, to say the least? The answer probably lies in politics. In the late 1980s, when the leak was first discovered, the CIA was going through a very sensitive time in the wake of the Iran-Contra investigations which had embarrassed it as the media got hold of the story. The potentially long search for a CIA mole, if carried out by the CIA itself, might have become a public relations disaster for the agency. There was also the fact that in the 1970s the CIA had been riddled with paranoia about potential Soviet moles. For these reasons, the CIA asked the FBI to carry out the investigation, an example of inter-agency cooperation.

The CIA would be criticised after Ames's arrest, however. The fact that Ames had been living way beyond his means for some time should perhaps have pointed to him sooner. It is estimated that he secured between $3.5 million and $4.6 million from the Russians over the almost nine-year period he spied for them, making him the highest-paid known spy in US history. It is probable that Ames did not receive all of the money due to him from the Soviets: there is perhaps more than $2 million waiting for him in a secret bank account somewhere, if he should ever leave prison.

Ames was not discreet about his lifestyle and his money. Colleagues later said that he had his teeth capped and began wearing designer suits, when previously he had worn very average clothes. He also bought a $400,000 house in Virginia, paying with cash, as well as the $60,000 Jaguar car in which he was arrested. His monthly home telephone bill was over $6,000, consisting mostly of calls made by Rosario to her family in Bogotá, Colombia. Ames also had premium credit cards where the monthly minimum payment was higher than his monthly CIA salary. His official earnings were $60,000 a year, but he was visibly living far better than his CIA colleagues, though the details were not uncovered until after his arrest. His extravagant lifestyle began to be noticed by the CIA, and in November 1989 a financial inquiry was secretly begun by the agency into his source of extra income. This inquiry was suspended because of budget priorities but was later restarted and finally completed in the middle of 1993, less than a year before his arrest. There is no doubt that Ames should have been monitored and vetted more closely by the CIA. In hindsight it's clear that colleagues and superiors did notice differences about him, but these observations were never collated. Many people held a piece of the jigsaw that would have pointed to Ames much sooner, but nobody had the whole puzzle.

There is also the fact that Aldrich Ames passed routine polygraph (lie detector) tests in 1986 and 1991, both taken when he was actively a double agent. He later said that the skills needed to beat the lie detector can be learnt, and his CIA training would no doubt have helped him towards that goal. It is possible that Ames is a sociopath, as he showed levels of vanity, selfishness and lack of understanding of the consequences of his actions – key elements of a sociopath, who lies without even realising it. But it is more probable that he simply learnt how to beat the machine.

The spying career of Ames is full of contradictions. He was certainly cavalier and careless in the precautions he took, but on the other hand he managed to kept his spying going for almost nine years while betraying dozens of operations and people. What drove him to trade his country's secrets for hard cash?

Ames explained his motives for spying for the Russians as follows: 'You might as well ask why a man with no criminal record might put a paper bag over his head and rob a bank. I acted out of personal desperation.' This was a sense of desperation that built up over years, and betraying secrets to the Russians was the way out, as he saw it. But not every person in a desperate financial situation would have acted as he did.

Firstly, Ames had a high opinion of himself and his perceived place in the world. Like the Cambridge spies John Cairncross and Kim Philby (see Chapter Three), he had an intellectual arrogance that made him think that he could outwit huge intelligence agencies, such as the CIA and the FBI. This intellectual gamesmanship would have given him the confidence to consider turning double agent. His primary motive was almost definitely financial (there is no evidence to show any strong ideological leaning towards communism), but it was his personality that enabled him to become a traitor. Many people faced with searing debts would have cut back financially or even filed for bankruptcy. That would have probably cost him his CIA career, but many others would have chosen this path instead of spying for the enemy. Ames thought that he could have it all: clear his debts and massively improve his lifestyle while keeping his intelligence career going.

The financial pressure Ames must have felt was acute. Faced with an expensive divorce settlement for his first wife, he was then married to Rosario, who had expensive tastes and little control over her spending. Ames may have feared losing her and so felt compelled to take extreme measures.

How much pressure Rosario herself put on him to do what he did is debatable. As stated earlier, she was sentenced to five years in prison and then deported back to Colombia, clearly indicating that she was not innocent. Conversely, the length of her sentence shows that she was probably not completely complicit in Ames's espionage. Of course, she was given more lenient treatment because Ames entered into a plea bargain with the authorities on her behalf: in return for confessing everything, Rosario was treated lightly. The charge against her was one of 'conspiracy to commit espionage', so she knew what he was doing, but probably not all of the details and the extent of it. However, spousal or familial pressure can be very powerful, as strong emotions are involved. For this reason, Rosario must take some of the moral blame.

The way that Ames decided to show his willingness to work for the Russians is also enlightening. He breezily walked into the Soviet embassy, which was a huge risk to him as a CIA agent who had no justifiable reason to enter the enemy's lair. But Ames's disregard for security had already been well established years before he turned traitor, in the way that he handled his administrative duties. Ames himself later called himself 'sloppy', and that is a fair description. The CIA Inspector General's 1994 report on the case states that as far back as in 1976 Ames was showing a marked lack of care in his personal security and towards CIA classified information. In that year, he left a case full of classified material on an underground train on his way to meet a CIA colleague in New York. The source of the material was named, and it could have been fatal for that source if the information had fallen into the wrong hands and the FBI had not got it back. Four years later, in 1980, Ames left secret communications devices on his office desk, and in 1985 he was reprimanded for leaving his office safe open. This lack of security awareness continued when he was in Rome.

Ames acted as if he felt himself to be above the rules and regulations followed by his 'ordinary' CIA colleagues. In a 1994 American television interview, Rosario said: 'I don't think he did it for the money . . . A great part of it has to do with wanting to prove the world that he is better, more intelligent. It was arrogance.' This comment must not be taken completely at face value, as Rosario obviously had a strong interest in distancing herself and Ames from the financial motive. However, it does ring true with regard to his mindset. Ames would have needed such arrogance to contemplate spying for the KGB while working for the CIA, an agency that had spent most of the 1970s and early 1980s paranoid about Soviet moles. Money was undoubtedly the main motive, but Ames's self-perception as a maverick mastermind allowed him to take the path of a double agent.

His skills and strengths at work help fill out the picture. As we have seen, Ames's CIA record sheet was hardly unblemished, but he did perform well for certain periods of time and kept being given responsible and important postings. His superiors valued him, and he obviously had good skills as a data analyst. He excelled at gathering and writing up information for intelligence reports when based in an office, as in Washington and New York. This area of work takes thoroughness and the ability to weigh different views about sources and about the implications of intelligence to reach a balanced judgement. Ames undoubtedly showed these attributes in his job, as he periodically received strong appraisals and won promotions. His security lapses were black marks against him, as was his ineffectiveness as a field agent, but his skills were sufficient to carry him through. Looking at Ames's CIA career, one thing is clear: he showed no willingness to improve or adapt to less than perfect postings. He did what interested and came naturally to him well but would not morph to fit circumstances. He was inflexible and selfish with regard to his needs and instincts. This was another key psychological factor in his decision to become a traitor. His desperate need for money naturally blocked out any moral or patriotic loyalties he may have felt.

Alcohol was also a key factor in Ames's story. As his first marriage imploded, he drank heavily. He was late for meetings and become generally less than professional in many work situations. He was a man under strain, emotionally and professionally. Alcohol is a depressant, and although it gives short-term relief from problems, it can make a person's outlook far more negative if used regularly and in large amounts. The vicious cycle then continues: the more depressed a person gets, the more alcohol he or she needs, and so the amount imbibed increases. Ames was no doubt emotionally dependent on alcohol by the time he started spying for the KGB. As early as 1962 he was arrested for drunkenness and by the early 1970s had to be helped home by members of the office of security because he was so inebriated at a CIA party. In Mexico City in the early 1980s, Ames was well known for his long liquid lunches. A year or two later, he left his CIA badge and other items at a sports event. In Rome, between 1986 and 1989, he would often return to his desk after lunch drunk, and he once passed out in the street drunk and had to be hospitalised. As late as 1992, just over two years before his arrest, he passed out at a CIA meeting with foreign officials.

There is also the question of whether Ames might have felt sufficiently disillusioned by his CIA work by the mid-1980s to spy for the KGB to spite his bosses. Ames said later in an interview from prison published in *The Nation* magazine on 11 September 1995: 'When Reagan was elected, I felt that the Agency had gone much more into the service of a political tendency in the country with which I had already felt very strong disagreement.' This was probably true, but how many employees of large intelligence agencies are not always totally at ease with the changing direction of operations policy? If Ames felt so strongly about this, the natural reaction would have been to leave the CIA, as John Stockwell did when he did not agree with the operations he was involved in when based in Angola. Instead of exiting in an honourable way, Ames sold secrets to the KGB for money, and a great deal of it, not stopping when his debts were paid but continuing to fund a lavish lifestyle.

The 1994 CIA Inspector General's report lists the reasons that Ames gave during his confession for becoming a traitor. The financial motive – with the pressures from his divorce settlement to Nancy and Rosario's high maintenance requirements – was given as the key factor. Ames also told the CIA that the fact that he could meet Soviet officials openly in his CIA work for reasons of 'cooperation' left him open to temptation, as did his diminishing belief in his CIA work. His final claim was that the initial meeting in the Washington diner, when he handed over the bag of initial documents (for which he was paid $50,000), was in fact an attempt to trick the KGB. He claimed to have believed that the CIA sources and operational details he passed to the Soviets were actually secretly KGB assets anyway. He added that he continued to supply more and more classified information because he felt trapped and there was no going back. The first few points are reasonable motivations, but the last seems a blatant attempt to justify his mercenary and selfish actions. It needs to be remembered that CIA agents died because of his espionage.

Could Ames have been a sociopath all along? If he were a sociopath, he would have felt little moral compunction or compassion. He would also have been able to beat the polygraph easily (sociopaths usually believe their own lies). Ames's work record and personality show narcissistic and self-serving tendencies, but it is unlikely that he was a full-blown sociopath. The interviews he has given show different reasons for doing what he did, whereas a sociopath would usually believe a line of thought and stick to it. Ames seems to be trying to justify his actions. He may have had a personality disorder, and this might explain his arrogant lack of care and dangerous risk-taking. But it is more likely that arrogance, financial desperation and selfishness created a dangerous hybrid when mixed together.

Aldrich Ames is the only spy we have looked at to have been mainly motivated by financial gain. Mata Hari offered to spy for money, but there is no evidence that she ever actually passed any secret information. Other spies in the twentieth century took some payment from their secret masters, but the amounts relatively small and not life-changing. Ames was greedy and continued to sell the information he was privileged to have in order to maintain a high level of living for his wife and himself. No ideological case can be made in his defence, if ever a traitor's actions can be defended, especially when people die as a result. Spies can be politically or emotionally motivated, coerced or blackmailed, attracted by the glamour and adventure or motivated by a bitter hatred of society. Ames was none of those to any extent. He did it for himself, pure and simple. But in the end, the results of espionage are the same: people are compromised, people die. The game goes on.

In the twenty-first century, intelligence is as important as it ever was, perhaps even more so. With the greatest threat now being terrorism, information is at a premium. As in any war, a real war, the Cold War, or a war against a terrorist insurgence, knowledge is power. Intelligence gathering is a game of chess, where pawns are sacrificed and taken, until the Queen is knocked over and the winner declared.

BIBLIOGRAPHY

Files

The Cambridge Five. MI5 Files. File PREM/8/1524, National Archives, Kew, London.

Fuchs, Klaus. MI5 Files. Fuchs interview, statement, contacts, all 1950; see www.mi5.gov.uk/upload/fuchs, Venona, 1944.

Hari, Mata. MI5 Files. File MI5(e) KV 2/1, National Archives, Kew, London.

Penkovsky, Oleg. CIA Files. File 1.3(a)4, released 31 March 1992; see www.foia.cia.gov/penkovsky.asp.

Philby, Burgess, Maclean. FBI Files. CD-ROM, BACM

Research; see www.paperlessarchives.com/ philby.html.

Reilly, Sidney. MI5 Files. File KV/2/827, National Archives, Kew, London.

Documents and Articles

Ainsworth, John S. 'Sidney Reilly's Reports from South Russia to Russia Department of the Foreign Office, December 1918–March 1919.' *Europe-Asia Studies*, 50(8), 1998, pp. 1447–1470.

The CIA Inspector General's Report into the Aldrich Ames Case, October 1994.

Corn, David. 'A Talk with Aldrich Ames.' *The Nation*, 11 September 1995, pp. 238–40.

The Denning Report: HM Government Inquiry into the Profumo Affair. London, 1963. Available at the British Library, London.

The Report of the Tribunal into the Vassall Case, 1963. Available at the British Library, London.

Wales, Henry. 'Account of Mata Hari's Last Morning.' International News Service, 17 October 1917.

Books

Andrew, Christopher, and Vasili Mitrokhin *The Mitrokhin Archive: The KGB in Europe and the West* (2000, Penguin).

Bearden, Milton, and James Risen *The Main Enemy* (2003, Century).

Blake, George *No Other Choice: An Autobiography* (1990, Cape).

Borovik, Genrikh, edited by Phillip Knightley *The Philby Files: The Secret Life of Master Spy Kim Philby* (1994, Brown & Co).

Bourke, Sean *The Springing of George Blake* (1970, Cassel & Co).

Carter, Miranda *Anthony Blunt: His Lives* (2001, Macmillan).

Chadwell Williams, Robert *Klaus Fuchs: Atom Spy* (1987, Harvard University Press).

Cookridge, E. H. *George Blake: Double Agent* (1970, Hodder).

Cookridge, E. H. *Shadow of a Spy: The Complete Dossier on George Blake* (1967, Leslie Frewin).

Cookridge, E. H. *The Third Man* (1968, Arthur Barker Ltd).

Feklisov, Alexander *The Man Behind the Rosenbergs* (2001, Enigma Books).

Howe, Russell Warren *Mata Hari* (1986, Dodd, Mead & Co).

Kettle, Michael *Sidney Reilly* (1983, Corgi).

Knightley, Phillip *Philby: KGB Masterspy* (1988, Guild Publishing).

Knightley, Phillip *The Second Oldest Profession* (2003, Pimlico).

Lockhart, Robin Bruce *Ace of Spies* (1967, Hodder & Stoughton).

Meeropol, Robert *An Execution in the Family: One Son's Journey* (2009, St Martin's Griffin).

Moss, Norman *Klaus Fuchs: The Man Who Stole the Atom Bomb* (1987, Grafton Books).

Neville, John F. *The Press, the Rosenbergs and the Cold War* (1995, Praeger).

Ostrovsky, Erika *Eye of Dawn: The Rise and Fall of Mata Hari* (1976, Macmillan).

Penkovsky, Oleg *The Penkovsky Papers* (1965, William Collins).

Philby, Kim *My Silent War* (2003, Arrow Books).

Philby, Rufina *The Private Life of Kim Philby* (1999, St Ermin's Press).

Randle, Michael, and Pat Pottle *The Blake Escape* (1989, Harrap).

Reilly, Sidney, and Mrs Reilly *Sidney Reilly: Britain's Master Spy* (1931, Elkin Mathews & Marrot).

Root, Jonathan *The Betrayers: The Life and Death of Julius and Ethel Rosenberg* (1963, Secker & Warburg).

Rosenberg, Ethel, and Julius Rosenberg, edited by Canon L. John Collins *The Rosenberg Letters* (1953, Dennis Dobson).

Shipman, Pat *Femme Fatale: Love, Lies and the Unknown Mata Hari* (2007, HarperCollins).

Summers, Anthony, and Stephen Dorril *Honeytrap: The Secret Worlds of Stephen Ward* (1987, Weidenfeld & Nicolson).

Van Der Rhoer, Edward *Master Spy* (1981, Scribners).

Vassall, John *The Autobiography of a Spy* (1975, Sidgwick & Jackson).

West, Nigel *At Her Majesty's Secret Service* (2006, Greenhill Books).

West, Nigel *A Matter of Trust: MI5, 1945–72* (1982, Weidenfeld & Nicolson).

West, Rebecca *The Meaning of Treason* (1965, Penguin).

Wexley, John *The Judgement of Julius and Ethel Rosenberg* (1977, Balantine Books).

Wynne, Greville *The Man from Moscow* (1967, Hutchinson & Co).
Yalkowsky, Stanley *The Murder of the Rosenbergs* (1990, self-published).

Other

The Spying Game. Various interviews. Directed and produced by Jonathan Martin. First broadcast on The History Channel in 1999.
Red Files. Interview with George Blake. InVision Production with Abamedia in association with Devillier Donegan Enterprises and PBS. First broadcast on PBS in 1999.